MW01017218

THE EPSILON HANDBOOK

Channeled by Thea

Edited by
J. Daniel Gaynor

www.EpsilonHandbook.net

THE EPSILON HANDBOOK

Copyright © 2010, 2012 by J. Daniel Gaynor

First published in electronic form 2010
First paperback edition 2012

ISBN-13: 978-1480047976
ISBN-10: 148004797X
LCCN: 2012921459

Front cover photograph by atomicjeep
Printed in the United States of America

INTENTION

This book is for informational purposes only. It is intended to provide accurate and authoritative information with regard to the subjects covered. The publisher reserves the right to alter and/or update the content at any time based on changing conditions.

This book is not intended as a source of psychological, legal, financial, medical or any other professional advice. If you require professional assistance, please seek out the services of a competent, qualified practitioner.

By reading this book, you acknowledge that you assume all risks associated with using the content, with a full awareness that you, solely, are responsible for anything that may result from putting this information into action, in any way, regardless of your interpretation of the material.

THANKS

Many individuals have contributed to the publication of this manuscript. In particular, gratitude is due to those who provided editing support, and to the members of our Facebook and Twitter virtual communities.

Thank you for your insights, suggestions and questions. This book would not have been possible without your encouragement and your wisdom.

CONTENTS

Contents

We are not human beings

on a spiritual journey.

We are spiritual beings

on a human journey.

Stephen Covey

Chapter 1.
Your Soul Group Epsilon

How to recognize yourself as a member of Soul Group Epsilon - The turbulence that has begun - The system of global illusion - Why you must develop awareness, intuition and the ability to interpret signs - Why we are interested in your affairs

We who are on the higher planes of existence look with concern on your development. You are magical, and yet blind to your essential nature. You are at the conclusion of a long cycle of soul evolution; it has taken you aeons and lifetimes to arrive at this point. Will you awaken now to your calling and to the role you must play? Will you activate the understanding that you carry within?

There are many of you now, at all ages and stages of human life. You look upon your world with confusion. You look upon the many imbalances and believe that you do not have the power to correct them, for you are ignorant and fearful of your true power. You are unconscious. You must awaken. This is now the time to implement the talents you have brought with you, which you have struggled in sometimes loneliness and isolation to bring to maturity. Yet you will not see your talents in true light until you have understanding of your purpose.

We will communicate in simple language that you will know in your heart to be true. Our interest is not in political factions or religious ideologies. Indeed you belong to all factions and nations, scattered as you are across the surface of the earth. You must understand that our messages are universal. On our planes, there are no nations and divisions. Your divisions are illusion. Yet we will explain why you have chosen your differences of identity for the purposes of healing and learning.

You will see now with recent uncoverings and global failures that your system of illusion is in severe disorder. Many will hope for the return to securities of the past, though you souls, who we will call Epsilons, have no connection to what is past. Indeed you have struggled to free yourself from your obligations to past events, from who you have been, what some of you will describe as karmics.

The time has come for a new resolution beyond the dimensions of your personal choices. Your resolution lies in the collective power of your soul community, in the light of understanding that where the individual merges with the collective in the service of a common destiny, the bonds of remaining karmics will be dissolved.

You must understand that though your status and wealth in earthly terms may vary to a great degree, from the soul perspective you are equals. You are brothers and sisters in the soul family. Some of you have attracted recognition and privileges from the wider community for your talents, and these of you have a special role to play as you have influence and you are visible. Yet those of you who may feel yourselves to be not-visible and not-influential must awaken to the realization that your camouflage has been an advantage that you have yourselves chosen.

As when the seeds of the tree go into the ground, at first there is nothing to show for their development, yet at this time the roots are formed for the tall structure that will grow, which will withstand the wildest storms. Your roots within your earthly communities give you strength, and you draw your power from the earth.

Now a time has begun when you will see many changes in the fabric of your global illusion that you will describe as cataclysmic and catastrophic, yet they are necessary and a consequence of the incorrect use of will. Truly your planet is a paradise yet you do not realize it due to the imbalances of greed and the failure to distribute the resources that sustain you. Many know this in their hearts to be true. The awakening you will experience and the turbulence on all levels that you will come to associate with it are indeed a function of rebalance and redistribution, though they may cause pain and lack of understanding.

Thus you Epsilon souls, who have access to the higher understanding that we seek to communicate, must play your role of interpreters and initiators to ensure the building of the bridge into a future that will, at first, be fragile.

Indeed your turbulence has long begun. The events in your nation of America, on the date known as 9-11, when the physical symbols of trading imbalance and warfare were damaged or destroyed, have been a form of awakening for many of you. This was a time in which you realized in your hearts that an era of the past, a period of unawareness and disinformation, had come to a close, though you could not predict the cataclysmic events and unending warfare that would result.

Similarly you have perceived the signs of natural imbalance, of tsunami and eruptions and leak-ages of your essential resources, yet you do not know the connection to the policies that create such catastrophe and to the failure of your global leadership to address these policies. You are waiting for change, indeed eager for change, and yet you do not understand that you yourselves are the change that you are expecting.

As you persist in the illusion that you are different from one another due to your association of identity with nationality or tribal heritage or religious ideology, you fail to perceive that it is only possible to heal your environment and reduce the turbulence you experience through recognizing your claim to a higher spiritual allegiance. Thus we say you must awaken to your purpose for, truly, the time is now.

Though many of you are not in contact with your conscious ability to interpret signs, as your ancestors could, we see you do not fail to realize that the material expression of the level where all human life is connected, what you call the economics, is undergoing breakdown. Your so-called finance crisis is a signal to you, a metaphor, that even though your supply of resources is essentially infinite, the incorrect use of will and the disease of greed inevitably leads to shortages that multiply beyond your control. This is the Law.

In response to this crisis of economics, you have witnessed how the very institutions whose errant policies have instigated the crisis have themselves drawn profit from the turbulence while failing to adapt their policies. There yet remains the opportunity to correct these imbalances and to evolve beyond errors of judgement which have been made. However, you do not see political will to resolve and repair for, truly, your political system is also broken.

We do not say this to alarm you although, in truth, if you are not yet alarmed by your circumstances then it is futile to communicate with you.

Indeed, many have even failed to interpret the sign that the date of 9-11 is itself your nation of America's code for distress.

You will perhaps question our interest in your affairs. In response we wish you to understand that there are members of your soul group who have chosen not to incarnate at this time so as to provide you with wisdom and counseling from the higher perspective. You are not alone in the challenges you face although, truly, we cannot control your actions, even if we would, and seek thus to influence your thinking beyond the levels of disinformation that you call media.

Your situation is now too far advanced for you to prevent the events that are to come. Our concern is thus to supply you with materials that will support your awakening along with considerations of how you may ensure your survival. Be aware that not all areas of the earth will be affected equally by oncoming turbulence, and your priority must be to develop your intuition to the degree that you will sense threats to your security even before they arise. This advance knowing is your birthright, yet you must activate and refine it. You will also require the courage and flexibility to lead a nomadic lifestyle if your situation requires it. Thus many of you will have already chosen experiences in this lifetime relating to sudden movement and releasing previous lifestyles that you have outgrown, though the separation has often been painful for you.

Do you understand our thoughts as we express them?

Some of your membership have invested much time and awareness in soul evolution and the conscious development of the talents that are your birthright. You will be unsurprised at the appearance of this information. However, since a greater number of you Epsilon souls will be unfamiliar with this type of communication, with the concepts we are imparting, we wish to first provide you with the guidance you will need to recognize yourselves.

Those highly evolved members of your group, you who have attained a position of spiritual and thought leadership, will most easily recognize yourselves through your affinity to the vibration of this material. You are already accustomed to thinking at this frequency, though you may not consciously be aware of the specifics of your soul group membership. You are tasked with the responsible distribution of our communications through the networks you have labored to create. We will provide more focused impulses to you through this channel at a point to come, yet you will experience an intensification of your own inner guidance.

In advance, understand this: some of you have become comfortable in your positions and unaccustomed to criticism and disrespect. You must learn the skills of communicative combat again. Your front-line position ensures that you will, truly, be required to communicate to loyal followers and skeptical observers alike instructions that, at first, may create disharmony and meet with resistance. The reserves of trust you have established will be tested. This is an element of the awakening process, though you will perceive it as discomfort and turbulence. Know that through this you will achieve a clarification of your closely held beliefs.

There are many of you Epsilon souls that have attained a similar level of soul evolution to the teachers and masters you elect to follow. And yet you are in an endless cycle of searching for the truth outside yourselves and seeking confirmation of your own awareness through recognizing it in others. The time has come for you to advance to your own mastership. Your study has been absolved with success. For the many tools and spiritual concepts that you have invested such time in investigating and integrating have now reached their fruition and you bear within you the structures for a new level of conscious community. In your hearts you know this to be true.

In particular your knowledge of the ancient wisdom of astrology will serve you well in anticipating the events that are to come. Yet you must become active with your predictions and overcome your fear to be mistaken. Know that your self-judgement to be not-ready is a belief that you have ch order to influence the pace of your evolution. This belief has become redundant. You may release it without delay.

For certain, all you Epsilon souls can be said to share a fascination with the supernatural and the fantastic. This has been your method of retaining your connection to the non-physical realm which you know to be a reality. There are many younger members of your group who are yet unconscious and who choose to keep alive their cosmic connection through involvement with comic books and heroes demonstrating unconventional abilities. Know that many of these abilities you admire are in fact your own, yet you lack the wisdom and permission to bring them to expression at this stage.

Other young souls will recognize themselves through their attempts to counteract the laws of physical possibility through unusual feats of boarding or biking. Though you have been told by your elders that such activities are useless, yet you know in your hearts that your extraordinary balance and bodily self-trust are the keys to achieving your purpose. You are not easily discouraged, and you are learning mastery of pain. Truly you are pioneers and warriors, though you are not yet recognized.

Still other youthful members of your group have become dexterous in the use of simulated games, many of which are placed in fantasy worlds at the far reaches of your imagination. Again we say that such skills are essential for the future that humanity is unconsciously creating. You Epsilon souls will recognize yourselves through your advanced ability to assimilate complex new information, to project yourselves into new realities, to move through different levels with your intuition. Yet you must awaken to your larger subculture and open your awareness to spiritual laws and truth, for your task is not to withdraw from society but to integrate yourselves with the insight you have gained from your virtual adventures. Your time will come.

We will speak to the parents among you: though many of you feel unappreciated because you labor at the difficult challenge of providing security and education for unconventional children, know that your efforts are the cornerstone of the new structures. Some of your children belong to your soul group and you have recognized them as they were born. Yet others are members of a soul group with differing challenges and existential themes; you will experience them as quite contrary to your nature and they will unnerve you through rejecting your values and your wisdom. Know that they are also fulfilling their purpose and accept that through them you are learning to understand your own purpose through teaching and nurturing and to practice the universal principle of non-attachment. We will focus on specific issues of family and child development at a later time.

Many of you are expressing your soul initiative through activism and entrepreneurship. Thus you represent the dynamic and revolutionary quality of Epsilon souls, for indeed you are the agents of global change in many forms. Some of you will identify your purpose in opposing established elements that you perceive as unjust and divisive, yet you must understand that this phase of your evolution is merely a transition.

Truly you are builders and not destroyers. You see already that the structures and policies you oppose are falling in disarray, for their time has passed. Learn to conserve your energies of indignation. You are the natural allies of the entrepreneurs, who already are experimenting with the new forms and structures, though the soil is not yet ready for many of the advanced ideas you carry within you. To both of these Epsilon soul expressions we say: patience will show you the path.

We will speak to the many artists and creators among your number. These of you have learned through your inspired creativity to open the channels to the higher realms of existence, and you understand at an experiential level what extraordinary energetic potential for the development of new ideas you are able to access. Many of you are integrating spiritual and metaphysical themes into the forms you produce, and you are yourselves surprised by the power of your work to influence your fellow beings though, in truth, they are challenged to integrate the insights you are communicating. We say to you: be cautious with your influence. You are experimenting with soul concepts whose time has not yet arrived, though it is close. Your challenge is to appreciate that you are healers and guides, and your creations are the fruit of your experiences in previous incarnations, which you bring with you into this lifetime. Indeed the true purpose of your revolutionary creativity will soon become clear.

In general we will say that Epsilon souls are non-conformers who seek to operate outside of the established structures. And yet, in truth, there are those of you who now find your purpose inside these very institutions whose demise will make way for the new. You are courageous, for you are attempting to reform the diseased structures from within, and yours is a thankless task because the sands are shifting beneath you. Yet you must recognize the value of your experience, for your understanding of what can not work is the basis of establishing improvement. Realize that your purpose lies in your growing wisdom and not in the external effects, for truly you cannot rescue what is already lost.

And we will mention those of your Epsilon brothers and sisters who are restrained within institutions due to an extreme expression of your revolutionary soul nature. Even these of you are fulfilling your purpose, though you be judged otherwise, through your painful and profound understanding of the shadow side of the path, which must be integrated and not avoided if you are to reclaim your potential.

You are many and varied, nor can we mention the myriad of your soul expressions, yet we trust that you will realize yourselves in the descriptions that we have communicated. You must understand that your variety is in itself your advantage, for you have awareness at the level of experience in all elements of unfolding life.

Yet you must now activate this awareness, for you must deal with the turbulence of war. Indeed the war has begun, though the channels of disinformation have led you to believe that it is contained by your technology. You must awaken and realize that technology itself is the war, that technology manipulates your channels of information. This is a war unlike any your planet has experienced, thus you do not correctly perceive it and understand the role you must play, for truly you are all involved.

Now we will speak in more detail, that you may sharpen and refine your understanding.

Adversity is the

diamond dust

that heaven polishes

its jewels with.

Robert Leighton

Chapter 2.
The War You Do Not Perceive

War is a change in the frequency of your reality - It presents you with opportunities to develop your guidance and to accelerate your soul evolution - It is necessary for global evolution that the policy of constant warfare be seen to be erroneous - The roles of technology and media - The effect on your warriors - The illusion of terrorism

We will speak in more detail about the cataclysmic events for which you must begin to prepare yourselves.

Please understand that we do not seek to alarm you when we speak of the experience of war. War of itself is neither positive nor negative. Truly if you can accept this, you will have the ability to use the cataclysmic circumstances which are now destined to happen to increase your self-awareness and your evolution. Yet you must recognize that many who will be involved in this experience do not possess your level of soul understanding. Thus you will be required to harmonize an amount of turbulence, pain, and lack of realization. This will be a significant challenge for many of you.

We will say that many of you Epsilon souls have experienced war in previous lifetimes and have an appreciation at the soul level of the opportunities and dangers that you face. War is simply a change in the frequency of your reality. Although even the word of war inspires fear, the coming events must not be feared. Fear emphasizes the cloud of illusion. You will succeed in using these events as an opportunity to develop your guidance and experience of yourselves. Yet you must take every opportunity to prepare for the coming events to prevent yourselves becoming affected by the frequency of fear and the irrational behavior of many.

We say that war is a change in the frequency of your reality. You must learn to see beyond the illusion, and to realize that the present condition of your planet is not a malfunction of your environment, yet results from the ill-motivated and unconscious actions of many. Truly you have become unconscious and self-focused. Therefore, there is not the will to resolve the serious problems that you face. A change in the frequency of your reality is necessary to correct the imbalances. While you possess the ability to consciously affect this frequency, you do not possess the collective will. Thus, the coming events will serve to mobilize and motivate you. You may choose to view these circumstances as an opportunity for your soul evolution.

Some of you Epsilon souls have chosen to develop in environments of warfare in this lifetime. These of you have begun to understand how the frequency of warfare influences your choices. In war, it is not possible to be unconscious. Indeed, you must daily question your values and your allegiances and your actions. You will realize that every decision you make may result in grave

consequences for you. Therefore, you are empowered to choose wisely.

We will speak specifically about the nation of
America. In the aftermath of the events known
as 9-11, the nation of America has existed in
a state of constant warfare projected against
external nations. This is a defense mechanism
born of unharmonized grief. You have become
accustomed to the reality of war in an abstract
form. We say abstract and mean that though
your country is constantly at war, the results
of the aggression perpetrated are not directly
perceived by the citizens of this nation. Indeed,
you have become accustomed to thinking that
the prosecution of warfare has no direct consequences for you. It is necessary for the purposes
of global evolution that this belief system be
shown to be incorrect.

Specifically, the belief that prosecuting warfare
by technology in external nations may protect
your own boundaries is erroneous. This constant
illusion of conflict without consequences has led

many to become unconscious. Yet clearly, the Universal Law states that the energy which you expend will be returned to you manyfold. Thus the irresponsible prosecution of warfare in pursuit of security can, in truth, only have catastrophic consequences.

Indeed we do not say this to alarm you, for in your hearts you already know this to be true. If a person of great power, in an attempt to make himself safe, were to launch attacks against his neighbors and friends, creating widespread damage and destruction and refusing to acknowledge the senselessness of his actions, how long would it take before his neighbors caused him to suffer a misfortune? And yet your nation of America continues to prosecute total war against a myriad of perceived enemies, without accessing the understanding that the number of its opposing forces is multiplying by the day. Indeed, this is true at both the energetic and the human level.

We will speak about the energetic level. America is a young nation of great spiritual evolution, yet it has been seduced by the guidance of the dark side of its nature. Truly, the leaders of this nation have become masters of disinformation. Indeed they have even seduced themselves by their own disinformation with the tragic consequence that they are convinced of the sanity of their destructive choices. There is no logic, either at your level of reality or at ours, of spreading destruction to create harmony. Nor can it be logical to attempt to construct nations through annihilating them.

You will say that this has always been the case, as with your long tradition of colony building. Yet you must understand that, in times of accelerated evolution, what you have taken for granted is no longer relevant to you as a learning experience. It is necessary for the continued spiritual evolution of the nation of America for the policy of constant warfare to be seen to be erroneous. Thus the citizens of this nation, who have unconsciously validated these errant policies through their broken political system, will come to experience first-hand the turbulence and chaos which they inflict upon others. The result of this will be healing and understanding.

We will speak about the human level. You fear war not because of the events that you experience, but because of how you will experience yourselves. The change in the frequency of your reality, and the dismantling of the general expectations of social behavior which follows as a consequence, dissolve the restrictions that empower you to guard over your own shadow side. Many experience this initially as a form of freedom. Yet, in truth, it is seduction by the shadow of your nature.

You will perceive this clearly in the actions of many of your finest warriors who have been involved in battlefields for the recent time. Gradually, there is an erosion of values. Indeed, you will seek to justify behavior that you know in your heart to be inappropriate, that the structures of harmony would never tolerate, because you claim that the situation demands it. Yet, in truth, if you will examine the mindset of warriors who for years have been involved with the atrocity of this new form of warfare, you will see in many of them the dis-integration of values and of the mental faculties themselves.

As the nation of America has clearly experienced in the previous conflict of Vietnam, it becomes impossible to re-integrate the shattered personal-ity, and to re-assimilate the damaged combatants into your society. This you have clearly perceived and yet failed to implement into your awareness. Yet, in truth, the increasing number of shattered and sorrowful souls at the heart of your society is itself like a virus in your community system. Through the eyes of these fallen warriors, you will not avoid an understanding of the consequences of the horror that is perpetrated, though many will seek to justify the sacrifice through consid-eration of their own safety. Truly we say that this disintegration will not make you safe.

We will not assert that warfare is to be avoided at all costs. Truly you have the right to defend yourself in justice through necessary means, yet with advanced soul wisdom comes an evolved appreciation of what is necessary. You have witnessed how many of the calmer souls among your global leadership were convinced of the just cause of initiating conflict by manipulation of the information. And now you perceive that the train of events set into motion cannot be called to a halt, for a culture of constant warfare has become established at the highest levels of decision. Indeed you will realize that significant external influence will necessary to correct this imbalance.

This influence you will describe as catastrophic, yet it is simply the backward flow of the energy of catastrophe, as the tide washes back onto the beach what you have cast out to sea.

It is imperative that you do not underestimate the power of your disinformation media to create illusion about the purposes and the true nature of the war in which you are all involved. You must realize that, in particular during wartime, your news communications have the form of propaganda engineered to deceive you into supporting with your energy illusory objectives and rationalizations.

You Epsilon souls have developed an ability to pierce the veils of illusion, yet we say to you that you must awaken to your abilities and activate your advanced soul understanding.

Truly you must begin to question the word of terrorism in the light of understanding and ask yourselves who in fact are the terrorists and what is their ultimate objective. Indeed the terrorism that is being perpetrated is the unlawful and unbalanced appropriation of your global natural resources. This, in truth, lies at the heart of all considerations of national security. For national security is entirely dependent on your unrestricted access to the natural resources that sustain you. Thus any illusion of contrary motives is superfluous.

In this new form of warfare, the warfare of propaganda and illusion, the sovereignty of any nation, and the rights of any peoples, are of secondary importance to the resources which that nation has at its disposal. As you awaken to this understanding, and realize that your global natural resources are dwindling as a result of the incorrect and unbalanced distribution of wealth, you will begin to realize that this is a war that cannot be won and can have no identifiable conclusion.

Yet, in truth, only through the stated aims of combating terrorism and defending security can your warriors be motivated to perpetrate this unending conflict and the citizens of the nations involved be persuaded to support the dishonest initiative. Thus, the cornerstone of this modern warfare is the control of the channels of global information. Many know this in their hearts to be true.

You will realize that you are involved in a new reality of warfare when you begin to examine the tactics and behavior of those opposing warriors from the target nations who use their bodies as weapons in an attempt to counteract the forces of superior technology. These explosions of people themselves are an indication that the culture of constant warfare has permeated the human structure to a cellular level. Indeed, as warriors have become weapons, you will appreciate the impossibility of preventing the retribution that is to come and of protecting yourself against the disease that has been created by the erroneous policies of your global governments.

As a cancer that appears in one portion of the body and spreads with invisible speed until the entire body is diseased, thus the virus that has been created may emerge unexpectedly at any place in your society with consequences that can be neither predicted nor controlled. Thus we say to you that you must develop your intuition, for your governments are unable to protect you from the consequences of what they themselves have initiated, and only the strengthened connection to your higher guidance will show you the path to survival.

And we will also say that the sickness of warfare that threatens you is one that has infected your own warriors through their constant exposure to their own shadow, which has been re-imported to your nations. Only when you understand that at the energetic level there are no limitations and boundaries, will you appreciate that you cannot erect borders to protect yourselves from the consequences of the energies you yourselves have set into motion. Thus this process of self-destruction has been underway for years already, though your disinformation media seeks to de-emphasize it.

We will speak about the role of technology. As you have seen with recent revelations about protected material, the very channels that you have set up to protect your security have become the instruments of insecurity. The result of this will be an increasing global awareness of the reality of the energetic level.

Your level of evolution has enabled you to create an invisible technological framework in which you are constantly connected to one another. This is a metaphor for your level of psychic integration. Thus, truly, it is no longer possible for you to withhold valuable information that protects your perceived national security. Indeed you will see that the nations you perceive as your enemies, the nations who you consider to be undeveloped because they do not have a similar framework of technology, are in fact capable of striking directly at the heart of your technological structures purely because they themselves are not reliant on the same technology.

This is how your advanced technology will become the instrument of your decline.

On the energetic level, your thought impulses have the power of the most advanced technology, though you do not consciously realize this yet. We say to you that the quickening of the frequency of warfare will provide you with the opportunity to develop your intuitive capacities, for the motivation for survival is stronger than your resistance to acknowledge the power that you carry within you.

Nor do we speak to the citizens of the nation of America alone. Another aspect of this new form of warfare is the significant involvement of mercenary armies and their integration at all levels of the global military campaign. The degree to which the citizens of your nation are involved in perpetrating the destruction is the degree to which you will experience the energetic backflow from their actions. Thus we say to you, you are all involved.

It is necessary and appropriate for you to use the intervening time to recalibrate your awareness and understanding. For this reason, we speak to you in advance of the events that are to come. You must awaken and become highly attuned to your surroundings. If you invest your energy in evolving your perception, you will become immediately aware when the unconscious infection of warfare has infiltrated your environment. You must realize that many will be attracted to the energy of conflict, for they carry matching energies within themselves that are yearning for expression. Thus, war cannot be said to be an accident of circumstance; it is an expression of nature.

Truly, your technological war over natural resources is a misguided expression of the natural resources you carry within you. We suggest to you that you examine the vibration of the personal resources that you hold and consider which energies you may release in order that you become harmonized with the higher frequencies that will ensure your survival.

I cannot do all the good

that the world needs.

But the world needs

all the good

that I can do.

Jana Standfield

Chapter 3.
Your Unconventional Abilities

Your varied special abilities will support you in achieving your soul purpose - You are capable beyond measure though limited by your memory of the misuse of power - Your telepathic abilities - Your gifts of dreaming and healing - Your skills with prophecy and astrology

We seek to impress upon you, in the light of our communication about impending cataclysmic events, that you Epsilon souls possess advanced capabilities that will further your capacity to secure your physical survival and spiritual self-development during the time that is approaching. Yet you must first recognize that you indeed possess these abilities, and then consciously activate them. We say that you have chosen to incarnate at this time and to participate in the process of global awakening that is underway. Though many will perceive themselves as victims of circumstance, you must understand that, truly, you are the architects and builders of the new future that you hold in your hands, as the Phoenix rises from the ashes.

We will speak to those of you who have invested time in the conscious development of your unconventional abilities and those of you who have not. Remember that you are brothers and sisters in the same soul family and that you have been accorded the responsibility of supporting one another. Your special capabilities are many and varied, and only in the recognition and harmonization of these abilities will you access the power to achieve your soul purpose.

These faculties that you now seek to bring to fruition, you have refined and developed over multiple lifetimes. Though you may not yet have conscious awareness of the power and possibility that lies at your disposal, be aware that the recognition and activation of these abilities is now essential for your survival.

We emphasize the correct use of will in the employment of these abilities. Though your level of soul evolution accords you great power to influence and affect the lives of your fellow beings, you will require the development of wisdom and insight to fully understand the nature of your responsibilities during this time.

Truly you are leaders and guides, and correct leadership from the universal perspective is dependent on your recognition of the limitations of your influence. You must understand that on your planet there are currently a number of soul groups in existence, some of whom will have purposes and objectives which you may perceive as contrary to your own. Yet it is imperative that you do not squander your energies on attempting to influence either the awareness or the destiny of those souls who have chosen to follow a different path. Free will is an essential component of the nature of your reality. Thus we seek to impress upon you that the incorrect use of your will and influence will result in grave consequences for you.

As you learn to recognize when your soul energy is flowing freely, and when you are encountering restrictions, you will be able to differentiate between those situations which you have the power to influence and those that you do not. Similarly, you will recognize regions of the earth that are receptive to the seeds of your influence, and those that are energetically unsuited to the essence of your soul emanation.

Indeed we say to you that it is precisely this degree of awareness and differentiation that will ensure your survival. Your powers are not given to you for the sake of manipulation. The task that lies ahead of you is to align yourself with energies of a similar nature, that your collective soul frequency may provide a form of protection against the lower energies of turbulence and confusion and insulate you against the undesired expression of your shadow.

Primary among your abilities is your capacity to communicate telepathically with the members of your soul group. This we can say is an advanced channel of thought connection, which includes your capability to consciously communicate with souls on our level of reality. You are able to send and receive images and impulses, and some of you have developed the ability to recognize words. We wish to impress upon you the importance of this form of communication.

Indeed, many of you have been experimenting with a method of instant communication using the technological possibilities afforded to you by your internetworking and telecommunication facilities. Thus you have direct experience of the reality of receiving and interpreting messages instantly regardless of your position on the earth. Yet we say to you that it is unwise to become reliant on these external forms of communication. Truly we have stated that your telecommunication and messaging networks are influenced by propaganda, and subject to the ultimate purposes and control of your global governments.

Thus we say to you that you possess your own internetworking capabilities that exist on the level of thought emanation. It will be advantageous for you to recognize and to develop these abilities.

Yet we wish to impress upon you that there is also dissonance and propaganda at the level of thought impulses. You must become aware that your very thoughts are themselves subject to manipulation. Thus a precondition for the successful implementation of your psychic communication networks is the ability to consciously recognize and influence the direction of your thinking. Many of you are aware of this, and have invested your time in the development of mental protection mechanisms through practice of meditation and mind evolution.

Indeed, it is only through refining your capacity to thus clarify and insulate your mental state that you will be able to determine which thought impulses you must respond and react to, and which you will not.

For those of who do not have the prior experience of influencing the quality of your thinking in the way we are communicating, we advise you to urgently seek out the tools and opportunities for guidance afforded to you by the thought leaders within your soul group. Your intuition will direct you to the appropriate facilities for your development.

We will speak about your powers of manifestation. Many of you, in recent times, have been drawn to experiment with the principle of creation involved in transmuting your thought impulses to physical matter. The facility to create in this way is an aspect of your earthly reality that was demonstrated to you by the Nazarene Master. Yet there are many who have failed to understand the true purpose of the Nazarene's demonstrations, and who do not consciously embrace this method of creation, which truly can provide you with effective solutions to your perceived lack of abundance and resources.

You must become aware that there are soul groups at the level of global government who have full understanding of this universal principle and yet choose to appropriate the proceeds of their manifestation mastership without communicating their advanced understanding to the mass of their fellow beings. Truly we say that this is an incorrect use of will, and results in an unbalanced distribution of your natural resources with the consequences we have indicated.

Indeed, there are members of your soul group at the level of thought mastership who have also achieved earthly wealth through the understanding and practice of this universal principle. To these of you we say, it is not only your understanding but also the wealth you have created through expressing it that you are now required to put at the disposal of your Epsilon soul group brothers and sisters. You must become the leaders in redistribution. Yours will be an example to inspire those members of your soul group who, as yet, are unconscious of the responsibility of their latent powers of manifestation.

You must awaken and realize that the conditions of harmony and comfort in which you have accumulated earthly possessions for purposes of self-gratification are now in transition. Indeed, you will now be required to understand the higher purpose of the powers of creation you have mastered. For truly you are builders, and your ability to consciously control the elements at your disposal is the foundation of the secure future you are challenged to construct.

Indeed we say that cataclysm and warfare will create perceived shortages, and the illusion of shortage will generate fear. Fear is to be avoided at all costs, as it is of the lower vibration and attracts the influence and expression of your shadow nature. Thus, to avoid the emotion of the fear of shortage, you will be required to develop and to trust your latent powers of manifestation. Further, you must harmonize your individual requirements with the overall necessities of your Epsilon soul community. There is no logic in accumulating resources without transmuting them to practical uses.

As many of you are already aware, your system of economics will undergo a heightened level of turbulence and through this you must understand that only when the theoretical possession of wealth transmutes into a practical expression of material abundance that benefits the majority, will you be fulfilling your purpose of seeding the earth with the elements at your disposal. We will speak more fully about your difficulties of economics at a later date.

In general we will say that the advantage of your challenging external circumstances lies in the compulsion to recognize the true power of your thought impulses. Truly you are able to communicate on a telepathic frequency not only with one another, but also with the animal and mineral kingdoms and the natural forces themselves. As you begin to understand the powers at your disposal, which are generated in the parts of your mind that you do not usually access, you will realize that there is no necessity for you to fear what is to come if you will exercise your birthright to responsibly influence your environment.

You must recognize that, at a soul level, you have incarnated not simply with extraordinary abilities, but also with the unconscious memory of times in which you have exercised your capability to influence and manipulate in a manner that was erroneous. We can say that many of you are spiritually wounded from the misuse of your power. Indeed this is why you have perceived your fellow beings accumulating wealth and privilege through the expression of their talents while experiencing yourselves as inhibited from generating abundance. Thus many members of your Epsilon soul group have achieved economic stability only at a later stage in this earthly life after experiencing a range of trials and learning opportunities in this regard.

We say that it is necessary for you to grant yourselves permission to come into your true power. Unconsciously, many of you are waiting for a signal to expand into your genuine nature. Thus the change in the frequency of your external reality will, in truth, provide you with the permission that you are awaiting in yourselves.

We will speak about your abilities with dreaming. You must begin to recognize that the realm of dreams is an inexhaustible source of your earthly power, yet there are many who do not appreciate this. The unconscious state of dreaming provides you with direct connection to the reality of other levels of existence. Some of you Epsilon souls have developed the ability to consciously control your dreaming, that you may transcend the limitations of your physical existence and engage directly with higher sources of inspiration and creativity. This is your birthright.

We say to you that during the time of turbulence that is to come, it is imperative that you consistently seek access to higher and clearer sources of information. Only in this way will you be empowered to penetrate the veils of disinformation and to counteract the confusion of the lower energies. Indeed, you must learn to activate the intelligence of the dream state, that you may thus commingle with your guides and counselors on the higher planes during your periods of physical regeneration.

Truly you bring with you an appreciation of the possibilities of the dream state, and the magical powers that are to be accessed there. In this condition, you may travel through time, heal, conduct communication over distances, and experiment at an experiential level with possibilities before they have become transmuted into physical reality.

If you would only understand, as your ancestors did, that your soul experience in the dreaming condition carries equal weight to that of your physical reality, you would gladly invest the necessary mental resources to master your conscious awareness of the dreaming level. Many of you know this in your hearts to be true, yet you experience resistance in exploring this possibility.

Yet as the vibrational frequency of your external reality increases, you will also realize an intensification of your dreaming state. You must become aware that, if you yourselves do not commit to achieving conscious mastery of your dreaming mind, that this is again a level where, in truth, you will experience manipulation from those who would seek to influence your actions, and you will be powerless to prevent their interference.

We will speak about your innate powers of prophecy. Truly you have the ability to predict forthcoming events in your external reality. For this reason we say to you that you must not fear the impending cataclysm. Yet your prophetic capabilities have been subdued for the reasons that we have communicated.

You must begin to recognize the patterns that govern your physical existence. As the planets and the seasons move in fixed rhythms, so the process of growth and decline in your civilizations moves along a predictable course. You have perceived that previously advanced civilizations have dissolved into the sands of time. Indeed this is due to a foreseeable misuse of will and the fluctuations of your lower emotions. Truly you are repeating and repeating the same course without accessing the understanding that would enable you to evolve. Thus you claim to learn the lessons of history without appreciating that you yourselves are an endlessly repeating pattern that moves through the channels of time.

As you begin to understand the mental and emotional rhythms that govern and influence the fluctuations of your earthly experience, you will recognize the position in the eternal cycle of growth and decay at which you currently find yourselves. Though the specific details of your earthly reality may appear to you to be different, your underlying soul lessons and the trajectory of your learning remain unchanged. Thus you may predict with confidence the events that are to come.

Again we say to you Epsilon souls that your advanced understanding of the spiritual science of astrology will serve you well in bringing your powers of prophecy to their intended expression. Truly you may harness the powers of the planets that move in their predictable courses. Indeed you must appreciate that the planetary energies are influencing every aspect of your earthly experience, and that you yourselves are the physical reflection of the planetary influences that you chose at the moment of your incarnation. In this way, you will consciously realize that harmonizing yourself with planetary frequencies in an intuitive manner is key to the achievement of your purpose.

Thus you may begin to align your intuition, your free will and the predictable energies of your environment to create enhanced anticipation of any circumstances that may confront you.

Many of you Epsilon souls have chosen the path of healing in this lifetime, and truly you have unrecognized abilities in this aspect. Healing yourselves and healing your planet are parallel expressions of a similar purpose. Yet you are currently influenced by belief in the irrevocability of decay and do not appreciate the powers of regeneration that lie at your disposal.

We will say to you that you cannot heal what is destined to decline for the purposes of global evolution. Yet you must begin to realize that, once the destructive energies of warfare and cataclysm lie behind you, you will experience an intensification of your regenerative capacities and the wisdom of how to implement them. This is your birthright.

Indeed you are the builders and the healers of the new dimension of freedom. We will speak to you of your advanced capacities for planetary healing at a later date.

Thus we seek to impart to you in this brief communication that the extraordinary powers you bring with you into this incarnation are granted to you in service of the fulfillment of your soul purpose. Many of you have identified your unique capabilities and labored to bring them to expression and maturity. We say to all you Epsilon souls, irrespective of your current level of development, that you are powerful beyond measure and beyond your imagination. In the coming time, you will permit yourselves to consciously realize and to experience this dimension of your truth.

We are so accustomed

to disguise ourselves to others

that in the end

we become disguised

to ourselves.

Francois de la

Rochefoucauld

Chapter 4.
Your Relationships

The challenges of your earthly relationships - The different forms of relationship you experience - Why you have chosen to experience abuse - Your themes of power and the correct use of influence - Why non-attachment is the ultimate expression of your soul nature

We will speak of your earthly relationships and the many challenges and trials you Epsilon souls have to master in this regard. Truly we will say that it is difficult for you to have fulfilling relationships outside of your soul group membership, as the nature of your soul energies is easily misunderstood and exploited. Indeed, many of you experience frustrations in your earthly relationships, as your manner of perceiving and interpreting events is often dissimilar to that of your fellow beings.

You incarnated with memories of the joyous and harmonious relationships you have previously experienced within your Epsilon community, and often you will find yourselves yearning for this essence of effortless soul connection. You will perceive many of your interpersonal encounters as lacking intensity and depth, for you are bound within a limited expression of who you genuinely are.

Yet you may experience a reconnection and commingling with the members of your soul group, both on your earthly level and on our planes of existence, while you are traveling in the dream state. Thus, as we have indicated, developing the capacity for conscious dreaming will prove extremely beneficial and regenerating for you on an emotional level.

You must recognize that many of the challenging relationships that you experience in this lifetime you have yourselves chosen, to enhance your understanding, compassion, and self-awareness. Truly there are no accidental encounters. The connections you choose to form, and the families into which you were born, have a specific purpose in your healing and development, and thus you should not be surprised at the sudden and unexplained disappearance of beings from your environment once you have integrated the lessons of that relationship.

We will speak about the different forms of relationship you experience: with your parents, children, and members of your earthly families; the friendships you choose; the relationships formed through shared experience in your working environment; and your encounters of a sexual nature. Truly you will see that all of these relationships have similar themes and challenges. You must begin to release yourselves from your attachment to the roles that other beings in your life appear to play. Once you begin to view the experiences of your life from a soul perspective, it will become easier for you to acknowledge the gifts contained in the different forms of relationships in which you participate.

In general we will say that many of the challenges you encounter in your earthly relationships are connected to the use and misuse of power. As we have indicated, you bring with you a definitive ambivalence towards the reality of your soul power. Thus you seek to experience yourselves as both powerful and powerless in a variety of different circumstances, that you may come to understand the correct use of influence and will and the true nature of your Epsilon soul responsibility.

Indeed many of you have chosen experiences in which you have appeared to be the victims of physical, psychological, and even sexual misuse. We will say that often such encounters have taken place within the framework of your earthly families. Such experiences of trauma have taken you many years to integrate, release and move beyond. Indeed you may still be involved in the process of forgiving yourselves and the apparent perpetrators of these abuses. Yet, as we have indicated, you have incarnated with the memory of previous lifetimes in which you yourselves were the perpetrators of a catastrophic misuse of your advanced soul energies.

Thus, in this lifetime, you have elected to gain an understanding of the emotional consequences of abuse from another perspective. You must begin to realize the value of these often-painful lessons that you have chosen. Indeed it is only as you begin to appreciate how deeply the roots of abuse penetrate inside the human organism, that you will truly recognize the importance of developing your awareness with regard to the correct application of your tremendous power and influence.

We say that you will discover, as you begin to integrate these experiences of your trauma, that the grip of remaining karmics will be dissolved and new reserves of energy and soul emanation will become available to you.

Truly you have gained the ability to perceive the unconscious patterns that exist within human relationships. Thus as we have indicated, you have often chosen an intimate experience of dysfunctional structures in order to examine how such interpersonal relationships may be evolved.

Though many of you will have chosen such experiences on the earthly familial level, the level of soul wisdom you have gained can be compared to those of your Epsilon brothers and sisters who are struggling within dysfunctional corporate frameworks, defunct religious organizations, irresponsible political factions or within any other human social structure which is characterized by the incorrect use of will and an erroneous application of power. Indeed you may perceive your circumstances to be different on the surface, yet truly the underlying lessons are the same.

We seek to impress upon you that though it has often appeared that you are powerless to influence your situations, indeed you have gained a fuller appreciation of your power even through your inability to bring it to expression.

Truly you are teachers, and you have at your disposal advanced capacities for communication and for accessing inspiration and insight. Yet many of you have chosen to incarnate to parents who refused to acknowledge the nature of your wisdom. Indeed, this you have also experienced as a form of misuse. You must recognize that you have incarnated into a time when your parents, caregivers and even educators were not themselves prepared to integrate the form of insights that you carried within you. We say to you that the soil was not ready for the seeds of your evolutionary nature.

The misunderstandings and unappreciations that you have encountered caused you to withdraw your energies from your environment and to doubt your essential nature. Truly many of you have experienced this as a dark night of the soul. And yet you are warriors and not easily discouraged. In such times, you have developed exceptional resourcefulness and cunning, and learned to channel your energies into invisible pursuits. You have trained yourselves in establishing psychic boundaries. Further, you have often succeeded in integrating yourselves harmoniously within the very structures that you yearned to destroy. Thus we can say that you are chameleons, for you have mastered the ability to be present in any situation and to project yourselves as you are perceived to be, rather than as you truly are.

Indeed, though you may have viewed your actions as dishonest, you must recognize that this form of initiative has insured your survival. You have developed a capacity to remain undetected within situations and structures that you were motivated to examine.

Thus we say to you that you have incarnated to fulfil a specific purpose, and indeed you have spent a significant portion of your earthly lives in a form of hibernation, in order to develop the internal structures, awareness and understanding which you will require to assume your mastership in the time which is to come.

In your parents, you have examined not only the correct application of will and influence, but also the structures of teaching. Many of you have incarnated with a higher level of soul wisdom than your parents. We will say that you were wise before your years. Yet you have learned to analyze your

parents' advice and counseling while understanding at the soul level that often you were better
advised to follow your own guidance. Thus you
have brought to expression the independent and
rebellious nature of Epsilon souls, though the conflict and rejection you experienced has often been
painful for you.

Those of you who are now parents, caregivers
and educators to Epsilon soul children will appreciate the value of the lessons you yourselves
have mastered in your childhood. For you have
developed the capability to influence without
compelling, and to recognize and nurture the
individual expression and wisdom of the souls
who have chosen you as their guides.

Thus the experience of parenthood will benefit
your own healing and the integration of your previous experiences. Truly you will recognize, as you
guide and motivate your children, that you have
the capacity to access insights gained from similar
situations in which you did not enjoy the nature of
support which you are now empowered to provide.

In this way, we say that you are transmuting your experiences of trauma into an evolved mastery of nurturing and an appropriate expression of your will and influence.

And yet there are those of you who have become parents to children with a differing soul emanation. Thus you may experience the relationships as challenging and lacking in harmony. You must release yourselves from the expectation that your relationships must always be harmonious. In your situation, the resistance that you experience in your children is in itself a gift to you. For you are learning how to develop yourselves through the challenges of communication. Indeed these of you will be extremely well placed to bring to expression the essence of your uncommon soul wisdom in situations where you may meet with general resistance and misunderstanding.

Truly we say to you that all the situations that you have chosen for your development have a specific purpose within the evolutionary framework of the Epsilon soul community.

Though some of you Epsilon souls have elected to incarnate into large earthly families, yet you have often experienced yourselves as different in nature to your siblings. You have undergone painful periods of isolation and aloneness. Indeed we will say that the experience of aloneness is common to many of you. Yet through this you have developed essential qualities of self-reliance, self-determination and self-awareness. Truly you can be hermits, who may not seek to have many close relationships on the earthly level, for you are learning to draw your emotional power directly from the source.

Yet you have been required to develop the capacity for integration. Within your earthly families, you have received the opportunity to observe your various siblings making choices from childhood and planning their paths through life. Indeed, this is been an exceptional resource for you to examine the relationship between aptitude, choice and destiny.

We will emphasize that brothers and sisters on the earthly level are merely roles that you have

elected to play. Thus, as with your other relationship experiences, you must not be surprised if
you fail to realize a continued level of connection
with siblings beyond your childhood, or even that
members of your family may appear as strangers
to you. We say to you, there are many soul communities in existence on your planet, and you will
not often experience a deep emotional resonance
with those who have chosen a different soul expression and purpose.

We will speak of your friendships. In general we
can say that, in many of the friendships with your
non-Epsilon soul group members, you have chosen
to experiment with issues of power, dependence
and non-attachment. Non-attachment is truly the
ultimate expression of your revolutionary and independent soul nature.

Many of your fellow beings are attracted unconsciously to the light of your unconventional soul
emanation, yet they lack a genuine commitment
to acknowledge and to integrate the insights that
you communicate to them. This you have often

experienced as a form of energy robbery that, in truth, has been stressful for you. Indeed, true energetic harmony within relationships is only possible where there exists a mutual openness for exchange and evolution.

Yet you yearn for connection and appreciation, which often has made it challenging for you to release these friendships once your process of learning has been completed. We say to you that you are attractive and fascinating, yet you must understand the limitations and repercussions of your influence.

Truly you will be able to identify the members of your Epsilon soul community, for the connections you form will be effortless, unconventional, and characterized by an equal exchange of energy, resources and insights, irrespective of the difference in your earthly ages. Such relationships you will experience as refreshing and creative and healing. Indeed, though many of you have suffered the pain of isolation due to incarnations into regions where your fellow Epsilon souls have generally not been represented, the opportunities afforded to you by your new internetworking capabilities have begun to reassure you that, in truth, you belong to a large soul community whose members are scattered across the surface of the earth. This we will acknowledge as a transient advantage of your communication technology.

Indeed in your role as teachers and guides to your fellow Epsilon soul group members, you will often generate a shared channel to higher sources of information that you would, as yet, individually have difficulties to access.

You also perceive what we will describe as a mirroring effect, in which you will recognize solutions to your own challenges and issues through acknowledging their reflection in your soul group brothers and sisters. Thus we say that you function as constant sources of evolutionary support and guidance to one another.

You Epsilon souls who have already integrated and realized higher levels of your unconventional soul potential have ascended to influential positions among your earthly society. You are recognized for your wisdom and evolution. Yet these of you are confronting many similar issues of the expression of your soul power, though you are experiencing them from a different perspective.

To these of you we will say that you are confronting the issues of dependence, non-attachment and the correct use of influence through your relationships with the large numbers of followers you have accumulated. You will acknowledge that many of your students project their own soul power onto you and thus attempt to present you with the responsibility for their own evolutionary soul choices.

You must begin to recognize that, in some cases, it is only through enforced separation and distance from the soul guidance you provide, that your brothers and sisters in the Epsilon community will be able to ascend to their own levels of mastership. This will be a significant challenge for many of you, for you have become attached to their devotion.

Only once you understand that non-attachment to the way in which you are perceived and revered is an essential element of your own soul journey, will you be able to ascend to the advanced levels of mastery and evolved leadership that you seek to attain.

We will speak of your relationships with your colleagues in the work environment. Although many of you Epsilon souls have elected to remain outside of established structures of co-working, and instead prefer to operate in a freelance capacity, yet as we have indicated are those of your number who are currently employed within the conventional working structures. Indeed you are represented at all levels of your earthly organizations.

You are fulfilling your purpose of analyzing the thought forms, belief systems, values and underlying emotional rhythms that govern the outward manifestation of these organizations. Truly you are researchers, and though you would often seek to identify yourself with the generally acknowledged purposes of these organizations that you represent, indeed your principal objective is to develop your capacities of analysis and perception.

We will say that these of you are most directly and intensely confronting issues of power and influence. You will acknowledge that, in many cases, your fellow beings are unable to consciously recognize the quality of your Epsilon soul emanation, though they may find themselves fascinated by the revolutionary ideas and solutions that you communicate. Yet truly within these diseased structures you will not find the quality of acknowledgment and recognition for which you are yearning. This is a source of frustration and disappointment for many of you.

You must come to understand that you are unlikely to be recognized for the true essence of your soul emanation, for many of these organizations are in fact managed or controlled by soul groups with purposes and objectives that you may perceive as contrary to your own. Thus you will see that often you are unable to advance beyond a certain position in these organizations, while your fellow beings of lesser talents and capabilities ascend to positions of influence.

We ask you to appreciate that, in general, it is not your purpose to lead these organizations, for their time of influence is passing. Once you begin to integrate your wisdom and to communicate this with members of your Epsilon soul community, with whom you share a common resonance, you will begin to fully understand the relevance of the varied insights you have accumulated.

For truly among your number you have all the necessary experience to establish inspired and evolutionary structures in all aspects of human society, as indeed will become clear to you at the appropriate time.

We will speak of your relationships of a sexual nature. In general we will say that many of you Epsilon souls have elected to participate in intimate relationships with fellow beings who do not share your advanced soul emanation. Yet the arena of sexual energy exchange is a profound source of learning and evolution for you. For truly your sexual energies are the roots of your power.

Thus you will appreciate that, once again, within the framework of your intimate relationships, you are experimenting with the familiar themes of influence, dependence and non-attachment. For during intercourse, a powerful bond is established at the unconscious soul level, which it is extremely challenging for you to dissolve. Thus you experience the themes of power and powerlessness through your emotions, and learn to appreciate the correct use of intimate influence and sexual will.

For truly the transmutation of your sexual will, and the associated power to influence your environment, is one of the most advanced energetic capacities that you possess. The commingling of your sexual energy is indeed a miracle, as you will appreciate given that it is through this form of energetic exchange that new life is seeded on your planet. Yet in general we will say that you suffer from a lack of awareness of your true responsibilities in this regard.

We ask you to appreciate that you are long involved in the process of re-seeding the earth with members of your Epsilon soul community. Yet you have often chosen partners who do not correspond to your true vibration, for the purpose of producing children who will master the challenge of integrating differing soul emanations within themselves.

You must begin to detach yourself from an erroneous perception of your earthly roles. As we have indicated, your relationships with members of differing soul communities are transient. Thus you should not be surprised that many of your intimate relationships lose their relevance once the Epsilon soul children have been born.

There are those of your community who have participated in a myriad of intimate relationships, and those of you who have generally elected to preserve your sexual energies for yourselves. Yet these are both expressions of the same issue. You are learning to establish appropriate boundaries, and to recognize when your soul emanation is being misappropriated for the purposes of another.

We say to you that is your ultimate objective to transmute your sexual energies into a creative force that will act as a generator for the advanced society you are in the process of building.

Those of you who have been fortunate enough to establish intimate relationships with fellow members of your Epsilon soul community will acknowledge the unconventional compulsive power of your connection. The combined emanation of your intimate union will be a source of deep fascination and jealousy for your fellow beings. These of you are on an accelerated path to bring to expression your evolutionary soul capabilities, for you are affected to a lesser degree by the dissonance that is otherwise an element of the sexual relationships you Epsilon souls elect to form.

We will say to these of you that you will experience issues of non-attachment, energy harmonization, the correct establishment of boundaries and an appropriate use of your extraordinary ability to influence one another. Yet truly, the issues that you face in these evolved relationships are supported in their resolution by a higher form of guidance to which you jointly have access.

Your evolved relationships lie outside the framework of conventional choices, and you will experiment with various structures irrespective of how they are perceived by the wider community. Truly you are innovators and pioneers, and you must not underestimate the influence of your shared emanation on all beings in your environment. In particular, you will have a powerful effect on children, who will recognize in your unconventional form of relationship the potential for evolution that they carry within themselves.

Indeed we say to you Epsilon souls, regardless of the form of intimate earthly relationship that you have selected to experiment with in this lifetime, truly you are individuals. Once you begin to recognize the true extent of your soul independence, and to release yourself from the perceived restrictions of the roles you have chosen to play, you will understand that all your relationships are a gift to your learning and your evolution, and support you in the acknowledgement of your true nature and the responsibilities which you seek to execute in this lifetime.

No price is

too high to pay

for the privilege

of owning yourself.

Friedrich Nietzsche

Chapter 5.
Challenges With Money

Your current system of economics is destined to decline - You may experience this rebalancing as chaos and crisis, yet it is necessary - Your evolutionary path will lead you into a new money consciousness - Why you have chosen certain experiences with regard to money - Your responsibilities to yourselves and your environment

You recognize that your system of economics is now in a crisis of transition, and yet you do not accurately perceive the consequences of the current rebalancing which, in truth, will affect every nation on the earth. For many of you do not dare to imagine an existence without the values and structures of your earthly money.

Indeed, you have even grown to believe that you embody the value of material exchange that you possess or do not possess, and the process of separating yourselves from this illusion will be painful for many of you. Yet we say to you that this is now necessary for your evolution.

The true purpose of your system of exchange is to facilitate the flow of natural resources, to enable you to sustain a healthy balance of life on your planet. Yet truly the system to which you have become accustomed is now in decline. For your essential resources have become concentrated in the hands of the few, who choose to utilize them for their personal gain without regard to the detrimental and catastrophic effect of lack of abundance on the majority.

This results in an energetic imbalance on all levels of existence, which affects even the perpetrators of the unhealthy concentration, though they do not appreciate this on a conscious level. Many of you Epsilon souls understand this in your hearts to be true.

For it is as though within the framework of a family, one sibling were to consume a diet of only rich foods and the finest beverages, while the others must be satisfied with the nutrition of the scraps from his table. And though it may be that those siblings with insufficient nutrients would show the first symptoms of ill health, truly over time the unhealthiness of his diet must damage him who fed himself full on the richest ingredients. Thus the imbalance of exchange would undernourish all members of the family.

Beyond even this, the emotions of guilt and envy, which indeed are of the lower variety, would gnaw away at the remaining structures of harmony and invisibly weaken the bonds of trust within the family.

Thus you now experience the deterioration of your structures of emotional exchange, both within nations and between nations, with the resulting turbulence to your social, political and economic systems and the weakening of your environment. You must awaken and realize that the differences you perceive between these aspects of your earthly life are illusionary. For truly everything is linked on the energetic level.

Indeed we will say that the disease of greed is poisoning the body of the earth itself.

Yet you remain unconscious of the degree of your integration with one another at the higher spiritual levels, instead preferring the illusion of division and the perceived security of superiority. Such illusion is a detriment to your evolutionary growth and the rebalancing of your environment that has now become necessary.

We will say that your dysfunctional system of values in exchange has become unconsciously accepted, just as you trade in paper and believe that it is gold. Thus the current insecurity that you experience on your economic level serves the higher purpose of evolutionary awakening, that the veil of illusion may fall and you may realize that you are all connected, and that the imbalances of your structures which are now being revealed have a catastrophic effect on your global stability. Only through the process of rebalancing, which you experience as chaos and crisis, can it be possible to increase the vibrational frequency of your environment. Indeed, this crisis is a form of warfare through economics, which is already underway though many of you do not consciously perceive it yet.

As you persist in the illusion that your individual value is linked to your monetary value, in truth this erroneous connection results in a profound misunderstanding of your purpose. For truly you are all equals, with differing abilities and talents, and yet many of your more evolved abilities do not achieve recognition, even within yourselves, for they lack economic appreciation in the eyes of the majority. We will say to you that, in the time that is approaching, you will be challenged to recognize the higher purpose of each individual and the contribution that your talents may make to the evolution of your community. This contribution is irrespective of the value of money.

Many of you Epsilon souls experience challenges with money in this lifetime, for as we have indicated you are experimenting with the magnitude of your soul power, and harmonizing the misuse of your energetic resources, which you have indeed perpetrated in previous incarnations.

In truth, money is a physical form of energy. Thus your ability to appropriately manage the economic funds at your disposal is itself a form of distribution of your soul emanation. We say that you experience yourselves as powerful or powerless depending on the monetary resources you have at your disposal. Yet irrespective of your earthly wealth, at the soul level the lessons you are integrating are the same.

We say to you that your evolutionary path will lead you into a new consciousness regarding the correct application of your economic exchange. Thus the difficulties with economics which many of you are experiencing are transitory. You must awaken and realize that, in your process of development, it is of no importance if you possess money or do not possess money. You may perceive yourself as experiencing the flow of money in the positive or in the negative, yet for you Epsilon souls this polarity is indeed an illusion.

Just as you do not place a differing economic value on the positive and negative polarities of the magnet, thus you must begin to free yourselves from the perception that your genuine worth and value is related to your economic position. For truly both debt and wealth are illusionary.

The essence of what you are learning is the value of exchanging the material force of your soul emanation, and you are exploring the circumstances that you attract through the decisions that are involved in sharing your energies.

You will appreciate that when you perceive yourself to be in debt, many of your fellow beings will demand money from you. And yet when you are in a position of wealth, your circumstances will be the same, yet you perceive them differently. Indeed you must come to recognize that, in all the circumstances of exchange, the lesson is one of appropriate energetic recompense and balance, which some of you will describe as karmics. Truly we say that, through your experiences with money, you are in the process of rebalancing energies both in this lifetime and from your previous incarnations. This applies to both the individual and the collective levels.

The exorbitant value that many of you place on the possession of money is directly related to the insecurity that you feel on the emotional level, and the disintegration of healthy structures within your communities. For you have come to believe that money itself is a form of insulation. Yet truly there exist on your planet communities where the economic value of every member is equal and differing structures of exchange have evolved which recognize and appreciate the true value of the individual, and the contributions that each member makes to the well being of the community. Indeed we say to you that your evolutionary path will lead you in this direction.

As you move through the different cycles of power and power-lessness that you have chosen for your growth, you are developing an awareness of those situations in which your true value is recognized and are indeed learning to appreciate this value in yourselves.

For those of you who labor in employments that you do not perceive as exercising your true soul purpose, and yet receive an excessive recompense, will not be fulfilled on the emotional level. These of you are learning that the abundance of your economic level is indeed no compensation for the poverty you experience on other levels of your being. And there are those of you who have discovered your purpose, yet you acknowledge that the structures and abilities that you bring to expression are indeed ahead of their time and thus do not receive economic acknowledgment in the eyes of the majority. Yet you are fulfilled in your occupations, and experience that the emotional satisfaction you receive is indeed greater than the value of your currency.

In this way, we say that you are experiencing and experimenting with the higher emotional and spiritual levels of your being, and thus releasing yourselves from the economic illusion which yet holds so many of your fellow beings captive. This process of evolution in the structures of economic exchange and the perception of individual wealth is indeed challenging for many of you, for your disinformation media continues to perpetuate the illusion that money is the source of true power.

Indeed those who have accumulated large sums of money have the possibility of influencing many of their fellow beings, yet as you Epsilon souls begin to acknowledge the magnitude of your unconventional soul emanation, you will discover a similar potential for influence, irrespective of the level of your economic wealth. As we have indicated, the appropriate use of influence and the correct application of your will is a soul group lesson that you seek to integrate in this lifetime.

Through your experiences with money, you are also given an opportunity to practice the universal principle of non-attachment. For beyond the illusion of security and the attraction of certain objects to which you have become attached, what is your objective in accumulating large amounts of resources? We ask you to look within yourselves and to question your motivation for the levels of abundance that you seek to attain. For truly to possess more resources than you require for your development is a significant responsibility and attracts consequences on the energetic level which you may perceive as unwelcome.

Many of you Epsilon souls have chosen to experience economic struggle and even financial collapse in this lifetime, for you are learning to integrate within yourselves the complex emotional responses that such experiences entail. Indeed, though you may have perceived such situations as unwelcome, you must begin to recognize yourselves as pioneers in this regard.

For you have developed the ability to see beyond the illusion which continues to confuse financial health with spiritual well-being, and thus you are extremely well-placed to support your brothers and sisters in the Epsilon soul group, and indeed the wider community of your fellow beings, who will themselves experience the difficulties of this emotional reintegration as the turbulence in your global economy reaches catastrophic levels.

Indeed it is the emotional attachment to money that has sustained your dysfunctional structures of exchange long after their appropriate time of decline. Thus we say to you that the current economic instability, which has permeated all nations of your planet, will result in the eventual collapse and reintegration of the individual perception of self-value. This is an evolutionary process that, in truth, will contribute to the rebalancing of your system of exchange and an increase in the frequency of your environment.

We say to you that, regardless of whether you currently perceive yourselves as experiencing wealth or poverty, you must not judge yourselves. Self-judgement places a veil across your higher faculties of guidance and inspiration. You must come to acknowledge that your financial experiences in this lifetime you have chosen for the purpose of your evolutionary growth, and that indeed your present situation is transitory.

Many of you will not fully appreciate the significance of the experiences you have chosen until you come together in community with your Epsilon brothers and sisters and begin to consider your individual life choices in the context of the advanced community you are challenged to create. For indeed, within your number, you have accumulated all the necessary knowledge and expertise to establish new structures of exchange and an appropriate system of economics which recognizes the individual contribution and higher purpose of each individual, and will empower you to sow the seeds of your soul purpose into the ground of your global community.

Thus we say to you, it is imperative that you learn to detach yourselves from the interpretations that your disinformation media places on the current economic turbulence. Truly much of this information is propaganda designed to deceive you. For the illusion of complexity in your financial systems disguises the true motivation of those who would seek to manipulate you and appropriate your essential resources for their own ends.

You must seek to focus on the correct expression of your soul emanation within the limited economic framework in which you find yourselves. As the frequency of your environment increases, truly you will discover new insights and abilities that will govern your potential to create the resources that you need for survival and self-development.

Thus you Epsilon souls have the power to become emotionally and financially self-sufficient at this time, regardless of the turbulence that your fellow beings may experience through their continued attachment to the values and structures of the economic system that is now destined to decline.

Faith is the strength

by which

a shattered world

shall emerge into the light.

Helen Keller

Chapter 6.
Understanding Natural Disasters

Your survival depends on the development of your awareness - Your advanced civilizations will begin to decline - This process will increase the vibrational frequency of your environment - Why you are aligned with the destiny of America - Why you must develop your ability to recognize frequencies and signs - The role of the different elements

We will say to you that everything in your environment has a vibrational frequency. There are many who perceive their lives on earth in terms of positive and negative yet, in truth, we on the higher planes of existence see only the energetic frequency that is created, as you perceive the colors in a rainbow. Indeed we seek to impress upon you Epsilon souls that it will be advantageous for you in the coming time to activate your ability to perceive your environment from our perspective. That is your birthright.

In general, we will describe you human beings as very self-focused. You recognize the solar bodies and planetary forms in your universe, and yet you do not realize the energetic connection between all varieties of cosmic life. Thus you cannot begin to imagine how the vibrational frequency of your planet affects the other planets, interplanetary life forms and events on the various levels of existence.

We say to you that you must begin to become aware of these cosmic connections, for indeed your very survival depends on your awareness.

Yet you persist in the same destructive patterns of greed and ignorance and wonder why it is that the environment that sustains you continues to deteriorate. For years, you have correctly perceived the environmental crisis, yet you do not understand either the true causes or the ultimate consequences. For you are life, as your planet is life, and as your ecosystem begins to collapse so, in truth, do you.

We have indicated that your current course cannot be corrected without external influence to increase the vibrational frequency of your environment. Indeed you will perceive this corrective influence as a form of catastrophe, yet only through radical changes in your values and behavior will you take the evolutionary step of understanding that may ensure a harmonious continuation of life on your planet for those of you with the will to survive these changes.

We say to you Epsilon souls: you bring with you the will and the ability to survive. Indeed, you have chosen to experience the changes in vibrational frequency, for you carry within you the memory of previous incarnations as members of an advanced civilization, and you have the potential to adjust your frequency at the cellular level. This is your expectation. And yet you must now awaken to this expectation for, truly, the time is now.

Yet you must acknowledge that there are many who will not choose to survive, for they lack the capacity to harmonize their soul frequencies in this lifetime. Thus we say to you that you must begin to practice the principle of non-attachment, to avoid becoming contaminated by the lower frequencies of fear and confusion that will be common to those beings without the potential for adjustment.

Indeed we say that the frequencies you are challenged to acknowledge pertain to all forms of life, and thus to specific regions of your planet. If you examine your history, you will see that, at times, entire continents have shifted in their earthly position and waters have come to exist where once there were mountains. There are many recorded examples of the redistribution of energy that you will shortly experience.

We seek to impress upon you most strongly that you must activate your faculties of higher awareness, that you may anticipate the regions of your planet that will begin to be affected by the turbulence of rebalancing.

You have grown accustomed to certain patterns of weather and predictability in the behavior of the elements and thus we say that you are unconscious to the potential for dramatic change that the body of the earth contains within it. Yet you must now begin to realize that, as the human body may adjust the supply of blood to a limb that has become diseased, so will the regenerative powers of the body of your planet effect an adjustment of life-supporting energy to those regions with lower vibrational frequencies, and a cleansing and reclaiming through fire and water will result. This corresponds to a re-harmonization of the emotional level of human existence.

You have reached a point in your evolution similar to that of other advanced civilizations that have suffered a decline. We will describe this point as one at which you have developed your intellectual capacities at the expense of your emotional and spiritual awareness. Thus you believe yourselves to be more evolved than, in fact, you are. For true spiritual evolution involves an understanding that your earthly actions have invisible and tremendous consequences on the higher planes of existence.

Thus you persist in developing and experimenting with weapons whose very presence on your planet creates the disharmony and lack of balance that you now begin to experience in exaggerated form within your societies. Indeed, as we have indicated, people have themselves become weapons, so deeply has the frequency of warfare and the utter disrespect for the value of life penetrated the human organism. Yet your disinformation media continues to perpetuate the illusion that such weaponry increases your security.

Equally, due to the incorrect and ill-motivated distribution of the natural resources that sustain you, you have become reliant on forms of energy so unstable that their existence threatens your survival. Indeed, this is a metaphor for the destructive thought forms perpetuated through your disinformation media, which are now so widely distributed and pervasive that you cannot recall them, even if you would.

As an illustration, we will speak of the nation of America, for truly this nation has become the global leader in the dissemination of disinformation through numerous and varied channels. This disinformation, which you will often describe as entertainment, is indeed a form of mind control and emotional manipulation of your fellow beings. Yet, due to an erroneous belief in your continued supremacy, and the infiltration of the shadow of your nature, you broadcast many visual thought forms that depict you yourselves as the victims of catastrophic attack.

You must awaken and begin to understand that, truly, you are thus exporting the seeds of your own destruction. Such insensitivity, arrogance and perceived invulnerability are common to advanced civilizations at the beginning of a period of economic decline and spiritual rebalancing.

Indeed we will say that you are so ignorant of the consequences of your actions and the turbulence that you are creating on the higher levels of existence, that you do not even recognize the illogicality of your own disinformation patterns. For truly, through the catastrophic situations which you choose to depict, you are revealing the vulnerability of your emotional responses and mental structures to your perceived enemies, believing those enemies to be insufficiently evolved to use this information against you.

Thus you engage in warfare that reduces your defenses and spread disinformation that advances your destruction, unknowingly fulfilling the cosmic Law that states: what you sow you will reap. A further instance of this cycle of self-destruction can be perceived in the recent uncoverings that have, in truth, exposed your motivations and machinations in political dealings through the exaggeration of the advanced channels you have constructed to protect their secrecy.

We will explain our emphasis on the nation of America. Those of you Epsilon souls who are citizens of this great nation must begin to understand that the immense power at your disposal, coupled with your ability to project your national influence through the channels of disinformation media, have resulted in your assuming the role of the protagonist in the evolutionary saga that is now unfolding which, in truth, will affect all the beings on your planet.

Indeed your nation has become adept at projecting qualities that it no longer possesses, and punishing partner nations for the perceived absence of these qualities. Thus we say that, in truth, your external politics is founded on illusion.

In particular, the values of capitalism and democratic process and the Christian religious belief, which you hold in high regard, have become distorted to such a degree within your own borders that you cannot reasonably seek to impose them onto your fellow beings. You must awaken and realize the limitations of your influence and the true level of your evolution. Further attempts to forcibly export these flawed belief structures will only exacerbate the energetic backflow that we have described. Truly this is a turning point in your spiritual awareness of yourselves. For how can you view the disintegration of your own economic, political, social and religious structures without achieving the understanding that the beliefs on which they are founded must be erroneous?

In this way, you hold the potential for the appropriate education and enlightenment of the wider mass of your fellow beings through the recognition and rebalancing of your own errors of judgement, communicated through the correct utilization of your advanced disinformation media. This is your evolutionary responsibility, though truly you show no signs of a willingness to accept it. Thus we say to you that, instead, you have taken on the role of experiencing the energetic backflow of your inappropriate actions, though this will be painful for many of you. Yet this will result in widespread learning and an increase in the vibrational frequency of your environment. Indeed these are alternative paths towards an identical goal.

We will say that all of you Epsilon souls, whether or not you are citizens of the nation of America, are aligned with the destiny of that nation during this time. For America most closely represents the behavior and profound spiritual learning experiences of the advanced civilizations in which you yourselves have participated in previous incarnations and, in truth, embodies the issues of the correct use of power and influence which you seek to integrate in this lifetime.

Yet the instances of rebalancing, which you will perceive as cataclysm and catastrophe, will affect not only the nation of America but also many points across the surface of your planet. Truly we say to you, you have the capability to anticipate these changes if you will activate your ability to consciously recognize the frequencies and evolving patterns of your environment.

You are aware of the four primary elements that exist on your planet: earth, fire, air and water. You must come to understand that these elements represent differing frequencies in the body of the earth that will seek to rebalance themselves, as indeed you seek to rebalance the mental, emotional, physical and spiritual levels of your own being.

Thus we say that you must begin to appreciate the particular frequencies of the events you will begin to experience, that you may understand the nature of the changes that are taking place in different regions and the energies that are being reharmonized. In response to these changes, many will be overcome by the lower vibrations of fear and confusion that, in truth, will negatively influence their ability to react appropriately to the turbulence. Beyond this, there will be those who will use the unfolding confusion as an excuse to release the energies of the shadow of their nature.

Yet we say to you Epsilon souls, you have the capacity to align yourselves with the natural forces that seek to increase the frequency of your environment and thus, in truth, it is not necessary for you to be in fear. Instead, you may choose to welcome the dramatic energies that will be set into motion as an external expression of your own soul vibration and the desire for fundamental change that you carry within you. Therefore we say: begin to align yourselves with what has become inevitable.

We have indicated that you must reclaim your ability to interpret signs, as your ancestors could. For truly there are events that have already taken place that provide you with a clear indication of what is to come. We will mention a recent occurrence, which you will agree is without precedent, that affected widespread regions of your continent of Europe. The substances expelled from an erupting volcano, borne aloft by the winds, became widely dissipated and, in truth, proved to be toxic to the operation of your aircraft. In this instance, as you have perceived, widespread chaos and confusion, in addition to substantial economic turbulence, resulted from a natural event that can be described as minor.

Yet there was no consideration in your disinformation media as to the causes and repercussions of such an occurrence at the higher levels of existence. Thus we say that you are unconscious, for you perceive the changes that are taking place around you and yet you lack the ability to consciously interpret them. In this case, you have seen a combination of the elements of fire and air, and truly you have been given an opportunity to understand the fragility of your systems and structures when confronted by the potential for dramatic change that the body of the earth holds at its disposal.

The element of air corresponds to the intellectual level of your human existence. Thus, in this example, we ask you to appreciate that the body of the earth is able to disseminate its own form of information that, in truth, has the power to render your advanced technological systems inoperable. Indeed we say that you must begin to interpret the signals in your environment in this manner.

And we will mention another occurrence, which took place near the shores of your nation of America. Truly you have perceived how a minor disruption at one of your technological installations resulted in an immense quantity of your natural resources mingling with the waters of the ocean in a way that you were unable to recover them. Indeed, though you have employed your finest intellect and every technological device at your disposal, you have been confounded by the elements that did not permit a resolution of the situation until the incorrect motivation, dysfunctional structures and incompetence of your operations had been brought to the awareness of a large number of your fellow beings.

In this case, you have seen a combination of the elements of fire and water. Truly we say to you that these events are minor in comparison with what is to come; yet they have revealed your general level of unpreparedness, the slowness of your responses and your inability to correctly interpret such occurrences from the higher spiritual perspective. Indeed, this particular event has demonstrated beyond doubt that you are bleeding at the emotional level of your existence, though you seek to merely refill the wounds without any profound consideration of why the patient is losing blood.

We say to you that events such as these are given to you as a warning of what is to come, and that you may come to understand that your global governments do not possess the ability to protect you from occurrences of this nature. Truly you must come to realize that you alone hold the responsibility for your physical survival and spiritual self-development during this period of time.

As you increase the level of your awareness and begin to consciously acknowledge the higher sources of insight to which you Epsilon souls have access, you will recognize the meridians and energy points on the surface of the earth which will become the principal channels for the cosmic forces of rebalancing. Indeed the body of the earth can be said to correspond to your own human physical structure, which many of you Epsilon souls have become adept at interpreting and healing in this lifetime.

Your physical body contains a network of chakras and meridians, which govern the harmonious and appropriate flow of energy through your system and, in truth, sustain your physical life. As you have come to realize, when these energy centres and channels become blocked or malfunctioning, you begin to experience painful symptoms in various regions of your body. Thus your physical system attempts to warn you of energetic imbalances before they threaten the survival of the entire organism.

Indeed we say that you must come to view the body of your planet in a similar light. For as you experience a lowering of your vibrational frequency when your physical body is diseased, so the disease of greed, the self-destructive thinking and behavior of humanity, and the incorrect distribution of your natural resources have affected the vibrational frequency of the earth body, and thus external intervention is now required to restore your planetary health. If you are able to view your planet in this holistic manner, indeed you will recognize that the eruptions and other occurrences that you perceive as catastrophic are simply an expression of underlying ill-health and an attempt by the body of the earth to appropriately regulate its energy flow.

As an example of your earthly meridians, we will mention the San Andreas Fault line along the western coastline of your nation of America. You are aware of the earth tremors that have repeatedly occurred in that region which, in truth, you have experienced as a form of vibrationary balancing. We say that it will be advantageous for you to involve yourselves in investigation, not only with regard to the location of similar meridians, but also as to the frequency of human activity that has developed along them.

In this case, we will say that this area of your planet is characterised by a certain intensity of interaction in social, economic and political affairs. Indeed you will recognize that many are attracted to this region to engage in combat in business, though they are aware of the existential uncertainties of this area of land. Yet, in truth, you will also acknowledge a high vibration of spiritual consciousness and an ingenuity of invention along this energy channel. Thus both the light and the shadow of your nature are illuminated by the regions of your planet which hold the greatest potential for transformation.

Indeed the vibrational frequency of your immediate environment is determined by the thoughts and intentions that you project upon it. Thus you will appreciate that, even in regions that experience catastrophic change, certain communities and even individuals will be miraculously spared from adverse effects, for they will be aligned with the frequency of the energies that are brought to expression. In this way, you Epsilon souls will come to consciously acknowledge that, in truth, everything you experience is a form of energy, as you have understood at a soul level through your adventures in previous incarnations.

Therefore we say to you that you must begin to detach yourselves from the incompatible belief systems in your environment and, in particular, from the illusory interpretations of your disinformation media. Truly you hold within you the capability to connect with higher sources of information and guidance. You must learn to pay careful attention to the behavior of your fellow beings, for they will unconsciously react to advance notification of events that are due to take place, though they lack the capacity to correctly interpret the intuitions they will receive and, in truth, will be governed by the frequency of the internal systems and patterns that they are unable to evolve.

Thus we seek to impress upon you most strongly that you must now act with discipline to employ the advanced structures of meditation, mind evolution, psychic defense and energetic balance that many of you have worked to develop. Indeed these are your survival mechanisms. In this way, you will be able to correctly interpret the frequencies in your immediate environment and your faculties for advance warning will be enhanced. Such motivated behavior must become your priority at this time.

Indeed this will allow you to modulate the frequency of your own vibration, with the result that you will attract into your reality those fellow members of your Epsilon soul group who have chosen to acknowledge your leadership and to follow the directions that you will begin to access though your higher communication faculties.

The fundamental changes we have mentioned will not come as a surprise to many of you, for you have interpreted the prophecies of the Mayan tribe, which indicate the relevance of the year of 2012. We will say that you are unwise to attempt to attach the process of rebalancing we have described to a specific point in time, for truly your perception of time is also an illusion, and the events you anticipate are already underway. Indeed you will find numerous references to the period that is beginning within your esoteric and religious literature, though you Epsilon souls may not identify yourselves in the imagery and underlying beliefs such descriptions contain.

Yet the date of 2012 has considerable significance, for many of your fellow beings have focused their expectations and their vibrations of fear towards this point in your earthly time, and thus you have begun attracting specific events into this frame. We say that you must not underestimate your collective power to unconsciously create what you fear. Yet you Epsilon souls will experience the forthcoming occurrences as a period of transformation, and you must seek to engender mental imagery that reflects and empowers the positive nature of your soul evolution. For the Phoenix rises from the ashes, and yet it is not advantageous to focus on the experience of the ash.

You will come to perceive the degree to which your disinformation media perpetuates the thought forms of self-destruction, and thus we say to you urgently that that you must choose and protect your own interpretation of the events that are approaching. Only thus will you preserve the independence of perception and the connection to higher sources of guidance and inspiration that are your birthright.

We wish to reiterate that you have no cause to fear the impending rebalancing, if you will awaken to the true nature of your Epsilon soul responsibilities and endeavor to become aligned with the essential vibration of who you genuinely are. Indeed, you will begin to experience yourselves in the enhanced manner that will result from a profound acknowledgement and acceptance of your purpose and the transformational events that you have elected to experience in this lifetime.

Mountaintops inspire leaders,

but valleys

mature them.

Winston Churchill

Chapter 7.
The Obama Presidency

You have come to identify with the personalities of your leaders instead of the soul power that they represent - Your political system is broken - You are involved in repeating cycles of expectation and disappointment - You are unconsciously awaiting a Messiah - You are challenged to recognize the true nature of the President Obama and that many of the issues he encounters are, in fact, your own

You have become accustomed to perceiving your identity in terms of national, tribal and religious divisions. This, in truth, clouds your awareness of your genuine soul nature and the specific responsibilities that you have elected to execute at this time. We say to you again that your divisions are illusion. You have selected your earthly identities, prior to incarnation, as part of your learning process to recognize and evaluate the different frequencies of your fellow beings and of the varied environments that you have chosen to experience.

You must now begin to understand the nature of your true identity as members of the Epsilon soul group and the advanced knowledge that you collectively share, that you may integrate and perpetuate the evolutionary changes that are already underway.

We will speak to you of the nature of your illusion. For, in truth, many of you remain captive to erroneous perceptions and projections of the events in your environment that cloud your ability to recognize your true purpose. In particular, you are challenged to question the way in which you perceive your fellow beings, including those you have selected to represent you on the level of global government through your flawed system of democratics.

You must come to realize that, through your political apparatuses, you are squandering your soul power and involving yourselves in endlessly repeating patterns of expectation and disappointment, which ultimately result in the stagnation of decision that you now experience. We say to you that you must awaken. Your continued attempts to shift the burden of responsibility for your current crisis onto your elected representatives is, in truth, a negation of your individual and collective power as members of the evolved Epsilon soul community.

For you have become unconsciously attached to your identities as members of disparate groups, indeed groups within groups, without acknowledging that, in truth, the extent of your divisions among yourselves ensures that it is impossible for you to elect leaders with a righteous claim to represent the majority. Thus the beings you propel into positions of national and global responsibility are indeed lacking your energetic support in the tasks you expect them to perform.

Beyond this, your disinformation media dissipates the energy of your focused attention and deceives you into concentrating on the perceived personality flaws of your elected representatives, which truly possess only minor relevance within the larger context of the enormous challenges that your planet faces at this time. Yet you will not appreciate the ability of your collective intention and thought forms to empower or obstruct the decisions that are made at the highest levels of your governments.

We ask you to acknowledge that you yourselves are responsible for the stagnation you perceive. For, in truth, your elected officials are nothing more than an expression and a reflection of your own evolutionary process. As you hesitate to shoulder the burden of responsibility associated with your Epsilon soul power, thus indeed you continue to elect representatives who indeed appear to be powerful, yet cannot effectively wield the tremendous power at their disposal. As they are, so are you; as above, so below.

Your illusion of division extends to all aspects of your earthly realm so that, truly, through perceiving yourselves to be separate from your global representatives as soon as they are elected, you unconsciously disempower them by failing to acknowledge either their true nature or the fact that they are at all times energetically influenced by you. Thus we say that you must become conscious of the integration that exists at the higher energetic levels, beyond the illusion of division, and begin to realize that each of you is constantly influencing the global evolutionary process through the extraordinary power of your thoughts and intentions.

If you would momentarily detach yourselves from your allegiance to your national identities, you would accurately perceive that your senior global representatives are, in truth, a small and insecure family of souls faced with alarming developments that indeed they struggle to comprehend. And yet they cannot even focus their full attention on seeking solutions that would benefit the wider populace, for they are at all times destabilized by the machinations of your disinformation media and live in constant fear of disempowerment and deselection by you yourselves.

We say to you Epsilon souls: you must strive to recognize your emotional patterns of expectation and disappointment. Truly you have incarnated in this lifetime to study the appropriate use of power and influence, and you have correctly recognized the limitations of your political processes to achieve fundamental change. Simply it is not possible for representatives who align themselves with a short-term office, instead of a lifetime purpose, to instigate and remain committed to a process of transformational change with effects that may be perceived by many as unwelcome. The essential nature of your political structures inhibits the correct motivation and selfless perception that provide the spiritual foundation for the decisions you understand are required. Many of you know this in your hearts to be true.

Yet you persist in the futile belief in the appearance of a political Messiah who will provide the solutions that you carry within you. Thus you project your own power onto various candidates within a dysfunctional system and react with fury and disappointment once your illusion is revealed. We say to you: this is an endlessly repeating pattern that has its roots in an incorrect interpretation of the teachings of the Nazarene. We will at this point refrain from an examination of the Nazarene's philosophy. Yet you must begin to appreciate the power of your disinformation media over time to distort the true nature of his message, with which many of you Epsilon souls identify.

In truth, the Nazarene did not incarnate for the purpose of demonstrating his power, but yours. He was a human being, as you are, illuminated and inspired by the cosmic energy that you describe as the Christ. And indeed when he promised to return, the correct interpretation of his words was that the energy he held at his disposal would return, and that the transformative and creative possibilities that he demonstrated would eventually be placed in your hands. Thus he sought to instruct the correct application of the universal power that is your birthright.

Yet you have come to identify with his person instead of the true nature and origin of his power, through a process we will describe as transpersonification. Thus you are trapped in the pattern of awaiting him and reluctant to acknowledge the reality that the cosmic power that inspired his actions now, in truth, lies at your disposal.

We will say that this unconscious and pervasive pattern of trans-personification has an exceptional influence on your manner of perceiving your fellow beings. For as you continue to await the re-appearance of your Messiah, or whoever is your designated prophet, you seek to elevate all those who demonstrate special capabilities to a position of worship, which we will describe as your disease of celebrity. Yet eventually, as you have often perceived, your artificial gods are revealed as merely human, as was the Nazarene, and thus you tear them down from their inflated positions and tread on them with the boots of your disappointment.

Indeed the latest objective of this unconscious procedure is your President of the nation of America, the evolved soul Obama. Truly you see before you a being with the ability and soul evolution to access great reserves of cosmic power to place at the service of humanity during your period of crisis and transformation. Many of you have recognized the nature of the energy that illuminated him during his candidacy, for you have been inspired by the vibration of his words and the integrity of his actions. And yet you do not appreciate that the power and potential for change that he embodies is, in fact, your own.

On our higher planes of existence, where we do not suffer from your illusions of division, it is not necessary to separate your global leaders according to the nations they represent. As we have indicated, we perceive your leaders as the members of a soul family with differing perceptions, experiences and abilities. Truly you are all connected, and during such periods of transformative change that affect the entire body of the earth, it is meaningless to focus on your national identities and priorities. For the oceans do not recognize your earthly boundaries, nor do the birds of the air.

Thus we say to you that the person of Obama, and the energies he represents, is a powerful and universal force in the process of your global evolution, if you would but realize it. We have no interest in political factions, nor do we claim that any individual is blessed with flawless motivation and undistorted guidance. Yet you are yourselves able to recognize the uncommon personal integrity, intellect, soul experience and global awareness that this leader embodies. Are you able to appreciate, when observing the development of this youthful President, that many of the issues of accelerated evolution and the correct application of power and influence that he encounters are, in truth, common to all you members of the Epsilon soul group?

You must begin to adjust your perception. Truly your democratic election process does not function as you imagine. As you focus on the anomalies of individual results and the machinations and dramas that lie behind them, you fail to recognize that, on a collective level, and irrespective of whether you choose to cast a vote or not, you are all energetically involved in the selection of a representative who will bring into being the destiny of your unconscious collective choices.

During the candidacy of Obama, many of you, regardless of whether or not you are citizens of the nation of America, have undergone a personal awakening and recognition of your true values and purpose. This we will describe as a global phenomenon, an appearance of the cosmic energy of healing and transformation that has led many of your fellow beings to unite behind the cause of hope and change, despite their differences in tribal origin, religious ideology and even political faction. We say to you: this is your evolutionary potential.

Indeed you may now wonder where this energy has disappeared to and if, in truth, it was merely an illusion. We seek to impress upon you that the energy has dissipated due to the simple fact that, once again, you have projected it onto the candidate instead of recognizing it in yourselves. And this despite the repeated mantra of the candidate that the potential for change is a power that you hold collectively. You have recognized the inspiration in his message and yet failed to fully integrate the true meaning of it: that for change to take place, you must change. And truly you are not changing by perpetuating the old pattern of belief that the Messiah must be the miracle you are not yet willing to be yourselves.

You must awaken. You fail to appreciate the extent to which your disinformation media distracts your attention from the evolutionary process that is underway through concentrating on the minutiae and trivia of your broken political process. Nor should you underestimate the ability of ill-motivated individuals and factions, within soul groups whose purposes may not be aligned with your own, to deliberately initiate your unconscious cycles of expectation and disappointment with the result that you are in danger of energetically betraying your own interests.

We ask you to acknowledge the unprecedented fragile condition of the nation of America, as evidenced by the increasing turbulence and energetic disruption at social, economic and political levels. Truly, as we have already indicated, this country is approaching a period of disintegration, the ramifications of which will extend to every nation on your planet. You must begin to recognize the nature of the global phenomenon that resulted in the election of the President Obama, and the external forces that participated in this unlikely event. You must seek to activate your ability to perceive beyond the illusions perpetrated by your disinformation media. Only when you begin to examine your own motivations for supporting and withdrawing your support for this representative you have chosen, will you achieve the level of clarity that will empower you to advance to your next level of soul mastership.

You have perceived a change in the vibration of Obama between his candidacy and his participation in the leadership role, and yet you are unwilling to view this energetic change through the eyes of your soul wisdom. Truly you prefer the seduction of your disappointment. Yet we say that you must pay careful attention at this time. For the lessons and challenges that pertain to this leader have exceptional relevance for the successful execution of your own soul purpose.

We have spoken of your Epsilon brothers and sisters who labor within the institutions that are destined to decline. These of you have an advanced understanding of the issues of energetic integration within inhospitable vibrations, and the resulting effects on your ability to project your own soul emanation. In the case of Obama, we say that it is possible to perceive how the clarity and inspiration of his campaign has become tainted by immersion within the political and social structure of the nation's capital which, indeed, he had pledged to evolve.

We ask you to acknowledge that your disappointment lies not with the candidate, but in the realization that the dysfunctional structures cannot be evolved, even by the application of the extraordinary energy field in which you yourselves have participated. As in your own lives you recognize the draining effect of your fellow beings who are unprepared to acknowledge the reality of your evolutionary soul vibration and instead seek to undermine you, thus you must begin to realize that it is not in the interest of certain of your global structures to evolve, and indeed they will implement any methods at their disposal to avoid the relinquishment of their influence. You will recognize that, in truth, the Nazarene sought to illuminate similar obstructions in his own lifetime.

It will greatly serve the evolution of your perception if you develop the ability to depersonify the political dramas that you see unfolding in your nation of America, and indeed elsewhere on your global stage, and instead begin to recognize the essential nature of the struggle between stagnation and evolutionary change that these interactions represent. Thus we say: you are all involved. As we have indicated, if you choose to succumb to the lower vibrations of frustration and disappointment, truly you will diminish your capacity to see beyond the veil of disinformation and to access higher and clearer sources of guidance and truth.

Indeed you will benefit from detaching yourselves from the specific policies that your leaders seek to implement at this time, and learning to recognize their essential vibration above and beyond the challenges they may confront. This is your evolutionary lesson. For you yourselves will shortly find yourselves in a situation where many of your fellow beings will be unable to correctly interpret the nature of your Epsilon soul vibration and the form of insight that you seek to communicate. Thus you will begin to identify more closely with the dilemmas of Obama and the difficulties of effecting change among those who are neither able nor willing to change.

We ask you to acknowledge that the global President you have energetically selected as a soul collective is thus a representative and an expression of your own evolutionary soul path, and that through your decision to commit to the process of change that he embodies, consciously or unconsciously, you are indeed presented with the opportunity to commit to yourselves.

We don't see things

as they are.

We see things

as we are.

Anais Nin

Chapter 8.
Your Spiritual Leaders

Many of your religious institutions have a hierarchic structure - You carry within you the blueprint for a different form of spiritual community - Your issues of dependence - What is the object of your devotion? - The nature and structures of channelling - The relevance of the case of James Ray

We have spoken of what we describe as your dis-ease of celebrity and your unconscious pattern of expecting a Messiah, who will initiate the fundamental changes that you yourselves have the responsibility to set into motion. We ask you to acknowledge that, truly, these attitudes pertain both to the advanced beings you perceive in your social, economic and political spheres, and to your spiritual and religious leaders.

We will speak to you of the nature of true spiritual wisdom, and we will seek to explain the structures of channelling cosmic energy, that you may recognize the qualities and abilities you perceive in your spiritual leaders and correctly understand the challenges you face in evolving these capabilities in yourselves. For truly you Epsilon souls are leaders and guides, and you carry within you the potential to enlighten yourselves and your fellow beings about the origin and appropriate application of the immense spiritual power that now lies at your disposal.

We have no interest in your religious ideologies and traditions, nor do we seek to evaluate the individual teachers, leaders and masters you have chosen to inspire you in your spiritual development. Yet we ask you at this time to call into question the purpose and nature of your allegiances, that you may expand your perception and increase your understanding of how cosmic wisdom manifests itself on your earthly plane.

You will appreciate that, in truth, many of the institutions on your planet consist of a hierarchic structure, which we will describe as imperfect and outdated. The essence of this structure ensures that those who ascend to positions of influence often achieve their promotion due to their managerial or political competence rather than the level of their soul wisdom. Indeed this applies equally to your religious organizations. Yet we will say that the capacity to manage is not the same as the ability to empower, and truly many of your earthly managers possess no interest in enabling their fellow beings to become more powerful. For thus they would themselves become redundant.

Indeed this unspoken power dynamic results in the development of institutions whose underlying psychological and emotional structures encourage dependence and inhibit the evolution of their participants, whose ultimate goal must be self-awareness and independence if they are to realize their potential. Many of you Epsilon souls will appreciate that the message of the Nazarene has become distorted for this reason.

Yet we will say that even among your number there are those of an advanced soul vibration who have been seduced by the level of their earthly influence, and who have thus sought to create hierarchic institutions that, in truth, are not harmonious with their purpose. For they have become attached to the unquestioning devotion of their followers. To these of you we say: truly you have incarnated to learn the correct application of your soul power and influence and, though you may have become comfortable in your positions, you will not ascend to your true mastership in the time that is approaching until you have recognized and corrected the energetic imbalances that your methods of leadership engender.

For, in truth, spiritual mastership is service, and you cannot correctly serve those who succumb to your influence by allowing them to project their soul power on to you and to remain unaware of the true nature of their independence.

Further we will say that you may not claim owner-
ship of the advanced concepts and philosophies
that have been communicated to you and placed
at your disposal by your sources on the higher
planes of existence. Truly you are messengers,
and the purpose of your message is to reveal
that the spiritual wisdom that you channel and
distribute can be directly accessed by the members of your Epsilon soul community, if they will
acknowledge their innate abilities to harmonize
with this frequency.

You must recognize that your true power lies in
your capacity to embody a correctly motivated
model for the behavior of advanced beings and
to demonstrate the appropriate use of cosmic inspiration, soul emanation and earthly influence.
For truly you cannot lose the devotion of your
followers who you have empowered to ascend to
their own mastership and to realize their spiritual
independence.

In general we will say that many of you Epsilon
souls are confronting issues of dependence in this

lifetime, which are an aspect of your learning the correct use of your soul power and influence. You seek either to depend on your fellow beings, or to be depended upon. In many cases, you will not be consciously aware of this dynamic until it reaches painful proportions. As we have indicated, you incarnated with memories of your level of interaction in soul communities on the higher planes of existence, where the divisions you perceive in your earthly reality do not exist. Thus you yearn to reconstruct this effortless commingling, without fully appreciating the importance of your individuality in this lifetime.

For truly you are individual sparks of awareness within the wider context of your soul group membership and the global community of your fellow beings. You have chosen your earthly situation and your life experiences that you may become conscious of your specific responsibilities and purpose at this time in your planetary evolution. We say to you that your independence is an essential element of your purpose. Indeed, until you truly understand the unique quality of your soul vibration through being able to exist in a state of energetic and psychic separation from your fellow beings, you will not appreciate the particular frequency that you contribute to the collective goal.

You will appreciate that, although the system of political democratics that exists in your more evolved nations may appear to encourage individuality of decision, truly your identification with parties and factions, and the belief systems and ideologies that they represent, involves you at an unconscious emotional level in collective rhythms and patterns that you do not accurately perceive. We will say that this tendency is yet more prevalent within the framework of your religious organizations and spiritual communities. For as you collectively strive to access higher sources of guidance and inspiration through your rituals of prayer and worship, you open yourselves to manipulation through your psychic faculties.

Thus we seek to impress upon you most strongly that you must exercise extreme caution during the upcoming time to prevent yourselves becoming unconsciously and inappropriately influenced by the frequencies of those groups to which your need for dependence encourages you to belong. Truly you must awaken and begin to question yourselves why it is that you belong to a group in order to worship, what is the true nature of that group, and what in fact is the object of your worship.

For we on the higher planes of existence do not require this form of elevation and devotion from you. We are devoted to you as brothers and sisters in the Epsilon soul community and indeed we recognize you as equals with respect to your soul emanation. Beyond this, we acknowledge our individual identities as aspects of the cosmic consciousness that has no object, as it is all encompassing and universally existent.

Thus we say to you: who or what is the object of your devotion? For when you come together to worship, you are accessing reserves of cosmic energy and directing these towards a specific end of which, in most cases, you are not conscious.

Thus it is that your Epsilon soul vibrations may, in truth, be harvested by unscrupulous individuals or organizations and be used to empower objectives that may not be aligned with your purpose in this lifetime.

Only when you begin to realize that you are constantly transmitting your soul vibration, and that the immense power of your thoughts and intentions always has an object, whether or not you may be consciously aware of it, will you appreciate that the current condition of your planet results not from a lack of energies for healing and transformation, but from a misdirection of these energies. We will speak at a later date of the specific role of your disinformation media in this phenomenon of energetic misdirection, yet you must awaken and acknowledge that your outmoded spiritual belief structures are themselves responsible for transferring your higher soul vibrations towards objectives that are illusory and non-supportive. Many of you know this in your hearts to be true yet, in truth, you continue to participate in this unhelpful transference due to your issues of dependence and your need to belong.

We say that you belong to the Epsilon soul community, which recognizes your individuality and your level of spiritual consciousness and the evolutionary role you have chosen to play in this lifetime. Indeed you will be able identify the most evolved members of this community through their ability to worship neither themselves nor external forces and objects, yet they are at all times inspired and empowered by the energies of the cosmic source. Truly this is the potential that each of you Epsilon souls carries within you.

You have become so accustomed to your hierarchical structures that you possess only limited awareness of the evolutionary blueprint for an advanced community that you are challenged to bring into existence during the period that is approaching. In truth, the images that empower your purpose remain buried at an unconscious level of your being, yet you may access them effortlessly while traveling in the dream state.

We say to you: in your imagination, you are walking through a forest. Around you, you perceive trees of differing ages and forms, each of which is rooted to its individual portion of soil. Truly it is not necessary for you to seek the leaders in this community of natural beings, nor do you have a requirement to worship one tree over another, though you may have your preferences, for you perceive that each of these life forms makes an equal contribution to the health of the community, and each is rooted to the same degree in the soil of shared consciousness. This is a peaceful and mutually supportive community of independent individuals with the collective purpose of providing an environment in which you, and many other beings, may replenish your spiritual energies. Such is your potential as a soul community.

Indeed you may use this template to examine the true nature of the religious and spiritual communities in which you participate for the purposes of your evolutionary growth and learning. For as you may not identify the first tree to spring up in a forest, so the truly evolved spiritual leader will prepare the ground for the fellow beings that will develop around him, and through his roots beneath the earth he will connect with them and encourage them to grow, yet he remains unconcerned if they should grow taller than him, for he has chosen and is satisfied with his own form.

In truth, each of you Epsilon souls is challenged in this lifetime to acknowledge the perfection of the form you have chosen and to trust the roots that connect you at all times with cosmic consciousness. This is your individual destiny, to become established as an individual spark of light that contributes to the radiance of your collective soul emanation. As you approach this recognition of who you are, you will be empowered to detach yourselves from the dependencies you have chosen for the purposes of your learning and growth, and you will begin to experience a mutually beneficial energetic flow with those beings on all levels of existence that share your evolved soul frequency.

Yet we say that this process of detachment will not be easy for many of you, indeed at first you may experience your individuality as a form of loss, for you have come to identify with your roles within the earthly relationships and communities to which you contribute your energies. However, as the vibrational frequency of your environment increases, you will experience an intensification and opening of your psychic faculties, with the result that inappropriate and unsupportive connections to your fellow beings will, in truth, impact your spiritual and even physical health.

Thus we say: you must awaken and become aware of the nature of the contribution that your Epsilon soul energies make to the process of evolution that is now underway. Truly you are required to question and to evaluate all the energetic connections that you choose to empower at this time. For you have elected to become channels for the cosmic energies of re-creation that seek distribution on your earthly plane for the purposes of reharmonizing and rebalancing the body of your planet. Indeed, you are yourselves energy centers with a power you cannot yet imagine to influence the events in your environment.

We will speak to you of the nature and structures of channelling. We on the higher planes of existence seek to communicate with you through the clarity of our thought impulses. Our perception of the events and circumstances that you will shortly experience is, in truth, unencumbered by the lower vibrations of fear and uncertainty that affect you on your earthly plane, and we are not subject to the destructive influence of your disinformation media and the illusions it seeks to perpetuate. Indeed, from our perspective, we recognize all the transformational events that await you as aspects of the cosmic consciousness that will serve your accelerated growth and soul evolution.

Since time immemorial, higher sources of inspiration and guidance have sought to communicate with channels on your earthly plane for the purposes of disseminating wisdom. Such channels are beings of advanced soul evolution who have developed the mental structures to interpret our communications, and who have the ability to access our frequency at will. We say that all you Epsilon souls possess the innate capability to function as channels of cosmic inspiration at this time, yet your success in this endeavor will depend on your ability to insulate yourselves from the surrounding psychic frequencies that, in truth, often interrupt this form of communication.

We may communicate thought impulses on an extensive variety of topics related to your protection and advancement during periods of transformative change. Thus you will appreciate that the evolved beings you recognize as your spiritual masters throughout your planetary history, including the Nazarene, have sought to instruct and demonstrate specific aspects of cosmic wisdom and universal principles to those with the readiness to acknowledge them. Yet we may only communicate this form of thought instruction to human beings who have developed the mental structures to interpret them.

Truly we say that, though humanity has often recognized the nature of the spiritual wisdom disseminated by such channels, indeed we may also choose to communicate at a similar frequency with your scientists, inventors, artists, educators, environmentalists and many other beings within your earthly communities who serve the function of energy centers, though you may not acknowledge them in their channelling activity and seek to make them individually responsible for the innovations they channel and contribute.

We seek to impress upon you that, in truth, your survival and advancement during the coming time depends on a reappraisal of your channelling capabilities and an understanding of your levels of integration at the higher levels of existence. For truly many of the ideas and concepts that you access during your lifetimes do not originate from your earthly reality, but are provided to you in service by your non-incarnate brothers and sisters on the higher planes. If you examine the history of previous advanced civilizations on your planet, for example the ancient Greeks or Egyptians or the community of

Atlantis, you will perceive a much more extensive degree of conscious integration between the human and non-human levels of existence. Yet this aspect of your awareness has diminished greatly in recent times.

Thus we say: you are all channels, and it is imperative that you awaken and begin to consciously examine the nature of the impulses you are receiving through your psychic faculties. For in truth you are being influenced at this level through your disinformation media and by sources on the higher planes of existence that may not be aligned with your soul emanation and purpose in this lifetime. The greatest power you hold at your disposal is the ability to consciously direct the enormous mental and spiritual resources that are your birthright, yet you may only achieve your goal through attaining clarity as to the nature of the information that you access and distribute. This process of achieving clarity must be your urgent priority at this time.

We will speak to you of another matter that pertains to your earthly spiritual leadership. For several decades of your earthly time, a process has been underway that we will describe as a re-evaluation of your structures of spiritual inquiry, what you will recognize as the consciousness of a New Age. During this time, many of you Epsilon souls have relinquished your attachment to traditional belief systems and have been inspired to experiment with various methods of accessing and interpreting higher sources of guidance and wisdom. Indeed you have invented or reclaimed forms of meditation, healing, teaching, dream interpretation, prophecy, astrology and the direct experience of non-physical sources that we will call shamanics.

Truly this period of time can be seen as a revolution in your spiritual awareness and, as we have indicated, certain of your number have ascended to levels of thought leadership which permit them to influence a significant number of their fellow beings in this regard. Indeed the development of your technological internetworking capabilities has greatly increased the potential for the dissemination of spiritual truth and cosmic impulses, yet we say that what you currently perceive is, in truth, just the beginning.

This so-called New Age consciousness or human potential movement has effectively reconfigured the value and belief systems of many evolved souls and indeed functions as a form of beneficial reprogramming and a reduction in the pervasive influence of your disinformation media. For you have learned to come together in communities that are not governed by a specific ideology and instead accommodate a variety of perspectives, beliefs and life experiences linked and empowered by a shared awareness of your energetic purpose on the higher planes of existence. This is your evolutionary potential. Yet we say that the existence of these independent thought communities represents a threat to the objectives of those soul groups who seek to enslave the psychic faculties of their fellow beings at this time and whose purpose you may indeed perceive as being contrary to your own.

Thus we say that you must pay careful attention to the case of the spiritual thought leader James Ray, whose actions or perceived lack of action during a shamanics ritual are currently under the scrutiny of the legal establishment in your nation of America. It is not our intention to offer an evaluation of the details of this case, for you may easily investigate the particulars of the matter yourselves. Yet we say that this legal process has significance for all you members of the Epsilon soul group. For if you examine the information in your disinformation media relating to this case, you will discover that many of the belief systems you have come to cherish and the life experiences that you consider essential for your growth and learning are themselves, by association, on trial.

If you elect to take an interest in the particulars of this investigation, you will have an opportunity to perceive how the nature and qualities of your Epsilon soul vibration, and the unconventional wisdom that you seek to disseminate during this time of evolutionary change, are interpreted by the wider mass of your fellow beings. For truly the belief systems engendered by the traditional religious hierarchies continue to hold sway, though their time has passed. Thus we say that, similar to the case of your President Obama, you may observe how the forces of stagnation seek to make irrelevant those who embody the attitudes of evolutionary change.

In truth, you may also examine the reactions and behavior of the members of your spiritual thought leadership at this time. For, as we have indicated, some of your number have become comfortable in their positions and unaccustomed to the rigors of communicative combat. Thus we say that, in the case of James Ray, you have been presented with an opportunity to become vocal and to defend the convictions and higher understanding of individual destiny that lie behind the events that are to be investigated, though your interpretations may initially result in misunderstanding and even ridicule. Truly you will experience this as a point of no return. For the handling and outcome of this trial will have far-reaching effects on how the essence of your spiritual consciousness and the specifics of your evolutionary work are perceived by the community of your fellow beings, and thus on your ability to reveal the true nature of your Epsilon soul emanation in the time that is to come.

The significant problems

we face today

cannot be solved

at the same level of thinking

with which we created them.

Albert Einstein

Chapter 9.
Your Disinformation Media

The invisible tentacles of disinformation media are rooted in all aspects of your earthly reality - You are controlled through the power of your emotions - You have become addicted to the manipulation - You must refocus your attention - The advantages, opportunities and perils of your internetworking technology

We will speak in more detail of the specific issues that confront you at this time due to the pervasive and damaging influence of your disinformation media, and seek to instruct how you Epsilon souls must now urgently adjust the manner of your thinking and behavior that you may protect your mental, emotional and spiritual faculties in this regard.

For as we have indicated, the immense power for positive change that you now hold at your disposal is primarily communicated to your fellow beings through the example of your behavior and the effect of the impulses you send out on the psychic level through the mastery of your mental thought forms. Thus, if you permit yourselves to be unconsciously influenced by the illusions perpetrated by your disinformation media, truly you are functioning as channels for those sources whose objectives you may perceive as contrary to your own. In this case, you will discover that the vibrational frequency of your Epsilon soul emanation has been re-engineered, and that your influence results in effects that you will with certainty experience as undesirable.

Thus we seek to impress upon you most strongly that you must now awaken and become aware of the degree to which the invisible tentacles of your disinformation media, and those who control it, have rooted themselves in all aspects of your earthly reality, and will manipulate your energies towards destructive ends if you do not take action to prevent this outcome.

You will recognize that we repeatedly and deliberately use the term 'disinformation media' to describe the conglomerate of transmitters which you will often refer to as news or entertainment. Truly we say that there is nothing new or entertaining about this form of psychic manipulation. Yet many of you have been seduced into consuming this unpalatable content, as children are persuaded to swallow bitter medicine that has been flavored with sweetener and given an attractive color. Indeed this form of medicine is damaging to your system and will not make you healthy. And yet we will not use terms stronger than disinformation to describe it.

For you must come to realize that, in particular, it is the strength of your emotional responses that is being used to control you. Your emotions are the motor that drives your behavior and empowers your thought forms, that they may influence the hearts of your fellow beings. We say to you: your thought forms are powerful, though truly your thoughts that are suffused with strong emotion constitute a force whose intensity you cannot begin to conceive. If you would only learn to preserve and to consciously direct this force, indeed you would begin to experience the kind of miraculous events that you do not yet even dare to imagine.

Yet, in truth, this emotional-psychic force that is your birthright is being harvested daily by the per-petrators of your disinformation media, and used to empower objectives that you will perceive as not being aligned with your Epsilon soul purpose in this lifetime. And indeed you must come to realize that, especially, it is your lower emotions, which you do not wish to acknowledge in yourselves and yet experience unconsciously in the trance condition engendered by many aspects of your disinformation media, which are being collected and used to control you.

For this reason, we do not seek to demonize your disinformation media, for truly if you begin to direct your emotions of rage and resentment towards this apparatus that controls you, you will only succeed in increasing the dimensions of its influence. Yet you may choose at any time to release yourselves from this psychic slavery by consciously selecting only those sources of information that support your growth and learning at this time, and removing your attention from the remainder.

For, in truth, that which you refuse to focus your attention on, irrespective of the plane from which it emanates, cannot influence you.

That you may begin to appreciate the tremendous power of your concentrated focus, we will offer the following example: if you wish to ignite a fire, you may stand with your twigs or paper in the light of the sun, the star which provides the most powerful source of heat energy that is available to your planet. And though you remain in the sunlight as long as you wish, truly your materials will not begin to burn. Yet if you were to take a glass that focuses the energy of the sun onto a particular spot, soon you would perceive an ignition taking place.

We will say that the sunlight represents the unquenchable source of cosmic energy that is available to you at this time in your planetary history, and the power of your attention provides the focus that may harness the energies at your disposal to ensure the desired result: the ignition of transformative change. Yet you stand in the sunlight of your potential and wonder why it is that the change does not ignite of itself. Truly we say to you Epsilon souls: you are the glass that magnifies the spiritual energy of evolution.

We ask you to recognize the degree to which your advanced soul energies are distracted, dissipated and misdirected by your earthly disinformation media. For truly much of what you describe as news and entertainment is a form of manipulation expertly designed to focus your attention on your lower vibrations and the shadow of your nature, with the result that you are unconsciously empowering what you least desire to manifest. For as you witness or imagine murder, suffering, hatred, catastrophe and all manner of situations you would, in truth, be horrified to experience, your lower emotional frequencies become stimulated. Thus you emotionally energize these thought forms and project horror into your environment with the full force of your soul emanation.

Beyond this, as many millions of your fellow beings simultaneously engage in this form of unconscious energetic transference, which is deliberately scheduled by the perpetrators of your disinformation media, vast fields of destructive energy may be created at will and used to engender disharmonies on the higher vibrational levels of existence. Thus we say to you: your thoughts are your environment, and as you begin to acknowledge that your environment is deteriorating and diminishing in power to sustain your physical life, truly you must realize that the catastrophic effects of disinformation are responsible to a greater degree than your industries and vehicle emissions.

We say that the time has come for you to awaken, to question what you are paying your attention to, and begin to realize that much of what you consider reality on your earthly plane of existence is, in truth, illusion. Your energies are being controlled and misdirected for the simple reason that you are unwilling to assume the responsibility for directing them yourselves. For you have become unaccustomed to correctly exercising your power to choose your experience of life, with the result that many of you have become passive consumers of illusory choices and concepts that are presented to you subliminally by those who possess no genuine interest in your growth and development.

We will offer examples: each of you understands intuitively what substances you require to sustain your physical health, and should you require direction there is ample information accessible in your libraries and via your internetworking systems, not to mention the advanced wisdom available to you at any time from your fellow healers and guides in the Epsilon soul community. Yet you prefer to be emotionally seduced by your various forms of disinformation advertising with the result that you nourish yourselves on substances that glitter without being gold.

You may have traveled to one or more of your earthly nations, where you have directly experienced that that the citizens of these nations, in their essence, are similar to the fellow beings you perceive in your familiar surroundings, though their appearance, customs and beliefs may differ in certain respects. Yet you allow yourselves to be influenced by alarming disinformation in your news media, which perpetuates the illusion that the inhabitants of these nations, who you have yourselves visited and commingled with, are alien and dangerous to the degree that their very existence threatens your way of life, and thus they deserve to be contained or eradicated, or that your security is dependent on forcibly imposing your way of life onto them.

When the time comes for you to make a decision about who you wish to represent you in a political capacity, you have the ability to tune into the frequency of the available candidates and thus to form an energetic picture of their respective soul vibrations. Instead, many of you pay attention to disingenuous disinfomercials, which seek to emotionally influence your choices through broadcasting fearful and negative portrayals of the possible outcomes. Thus, after months of such manipulation, you become so confused that, in truth, you are incapable of deciding appropriately.

Indeed these and similar forms of ill-motivated influence on your process of reaching decisions have permeated all aspects of your earthly reality. Many of you know this in your hearts to be true. And yet we will say that this manipulation has itself become an addiction, for you are fascinated by the energies that are stimulated in the shadow of your nature. Thus you find yourselves imprisoned in a dynamic where your moral and religious structures prohibit and demonize emotions and experiences in which you may participate freely through the channels of your disinformation media. Truly such methods of perpetrating illusion have separated you from the awareness of your genuine nature and now seek to prevent you from reclaiming the power of your Epsilon soul vibration.

We will say that, once again, your captivity to the influence of your disinformation media is another expression of the issue of power and powerlessness that you Epsilon souls have sought to experience and harmonize in this lifetime. For truly, in incarnations that you do not consciously remember, you have yourselves wielded extraordinary influence over the minds and decision-making processes of your fellow beings, with undesired and indeed catastrophic consequences that have scarred you at a soul level. Thus you hesitate to reclaim this element of your power, and instead experience the frustration that results as these methods of advanced manipulation are now used against you.

The time has come for you to forgive yourselves for your mistakes. You now have access to higher understanding, through which you will realize that the misappropriation of your soul power was a necessary stage in your process of learning how to express your influence appropriately. You have undergone a lengthy period of healing and re-evaluation, which has taken you lifetimes to complete.

Thus you now appreciate at the deepest level of your being that all forms of communication are, in truth, manipulative and that employing your wisdom to manipulate for beneficial purposes is the challenge that confronts you in this period of your planetary evolution.

Yet indeed there are many of your number who have already begun to experiment with your soul influence using the channels of your internetworking technology. For you have understood that such advanced channels, in truth, represent an evolution in democratic communication, though they exist as a counterculture within the overall framework of your disinformation media. We have indicated that the mastery you are developing in the use of these channels is a transitory stage in the establishment of your psychic networking faculties, yet it permits direct experience of the challenges and issues you will face in influencing and guiding significant numbers of your fellow beings, who find themselves intuitively attracted to the unusual frequency of your Epsilon soul emanation.

We will speak of the advantages and opportunities of your inter-networking technology. Truly each of you is now afforded the ability to connect instantaneously with the mental faculties of your fellow beings, wherever they exist on your planet, and to disseminate information in the form of written, visual and aural impulses that you may consciously structure as you please. We say to you that, through this global internetworking framework, you may recognize and unite with your brothers and sisters in the Epsilon soul family and begin your work of establishing the communication structures that will sustain your vibrational frequency during the time that is to come.

Indeed there is no further cause for you to experience yourselves as detached and disempowered, though as we have indicated you may have chosen your isolation and periods of disconnection for the purposes of establishing your individuality, affirming your particular frequency and developing your psychic independence from those communities whose vibration is non-supportive for your growth. Yet, in truth, you now possess the option of existing in energetically harmonious and naturally empowering regions, at a physical distance from your fellow beings if you require it, and yet remaining connected, inspired and informed by the members of your Epsilon soul community. This we will acknowledge as a transitory advantage of your disinformation media technology.

We will also say that the structures of your new internetworking systems confer upon you the additional benefit of anonymity. For reasons we have indicated, many of you are reluctant to express the true nature of your advanced Epsilon soul emanation within the physical communities of your fellow beings, and your life experiences have taught you to be cautious in revealing yourselves. Indeed you bring with you memories of persecution that you have endured in previous incarnations. Yet we seek to reassure you that your hesitation and caution is appropriate, for the moment of your full energetic expression is not at hand, though it is close.

Yet you must begin to appreciate that the cosmic power you may access through your mental and psychic faculties, in truth, allows you to influence the events in your environment without revealing yourselves. Many of you will find it challenging to recognize and to accept this aspect of your evolutionary consciousness, and yet your internetworking technology provides you with the opportunity to experiment with this very reality: you may easily accumulate large numbers of adherents and followers whose decisions, emotional processes and spiritual development you can significantly influence, even though they may never see your face or know your given name.

We seek to impress upon you that your internetworking technology is, in truth, merely a metaphor and a testing ground for the psychic networks you are in the process of establishing. Thus you continue to explore your incarnational theme of the correct use of power and influence, through experimenting with the ways in which you exert your psychic influence and, in turn, are influenced by others within your online realms.

And indeed you are also learning to acknowledge the reality of your interaction on all the energetic levels of existence, for truly there are many of you who have chosen the experience of establishing emotional connections with your fellow beings within virtual communities, though you have never encountered them in the traditional sense, and are unable or unwilling to disengage such connections for significant periods after you have disconnected your internetworking technology.

You find yourselves at a unique moment in your planet's history. For you have the ability, without effort or even leaving your place of residence, to communicate your wisdom and to share your Epsilon soul vibration with significant numbers of your fellow beings. Are you aware of the potential for change that now lies at your disposal? Yet many of you elect to use your advanced internetworking structures to communicate information that has no spiritual or evolutionary relevance and, in truth, merely serves to perpetrate the illusory concepts and values that are common to other aspects of your disinformation media.

Thus we say: you have unconsciously become distributors of the virus of disinformation. Truly you must now awaken and begin to evaluate the vibrational frequency of the content you choose to distribute. The lessons you are challenged to learn through the application of your internetworking technology will greatly serve you in your function as energy centers and channels of cosmic awareness in the energetic rebalancing that is shortly to take place. Yet, in truth, you will only learn these essential lessons if you become conscious of your behavior and recognize that all your electronic communication methods result in the dissemination of thought forms that can easily multiply beyond your control. This you describe as a viral effect, and truly your Epsilon thought forms have the power of your earthly viruses to damage and destroy, if you do not employ them with great care and consciousness.

Further we seek to remind you that the level of direct interaction common to your internetworking technology increases your psychic vulnerability and thus makes you yet more susceptible to the methods of mind control exercised by certain elements of your disinformation media that have also penetrated the virtual realms. You must realize that when you are engaged in online activity, you have established a direct connection to your global consciousness and may thus be infiltrated by forms of destructive manipulation that cannot be broadcast through the conventional channels of disinformation. In short, we will say that you are at all times in contact with the shadow of your nature through the material to which you have access.

We seek to impress upon you most urgently that, in the time that is approaching, you must exercise great caution in the use of your advanced internetworking technology. As we have indicated, the war in which you are all involved is technological in nature, and indeed there exist many weapons of psychic propaganda that have been developed by your global governments, which have the ability to manipulate your mental faculties and to encourage you to engage in behavior that you will perceive as contrary to your purpose in this lifetime. Truly we say that you must awaken, for you are subject to influences beyond your imagination and beneath the level of your conscious awareness.

Thus, in truth, we advise you to participate in online activity only when you have clarity as to the specific purpose of the energetic transactions you wish to initiate in the virtual realm. Indeed you have gained valuable experience with regard to these invisible transactions during your process of learning to communicate, develop and evaluate mental and emotionally-empowered thought forms in your online environment. You must recognize that this process has not been for the purposes of your entertainment. You are spiritual warriors in an information war the like of which your planet has never seen and, as evolved Epsilon souls, you have specific responsibilities to disseminate forms of cosmic understanding and guidance that may support and empower the process of rebalancing and evolutionary change that is now underway.

Indeed we say that, at this stage of your development, your advanced internetworking technology is truly the most powerful evolutionary tool you hold at your disposal for the purpose of disseminating your Epsilon soul frequencies. We ask that you do not repeat the mistake of underestimating the potential and misinterpreting the objective of your communication technologies for, in truth, you would once again perceive the results of an unconscious misdirection of your soul power as most unwelcome to you.

All growth is

a leap in the dark,

a spontaneous,

unpremeditated act

without the benefit of experience.

Henry Miller

Chapter 10.
Deprogramming Yourself

You have chosen your programs and experiences in this lifetime for the purposes of your evolutionary growth - You must begin to forgive yourselves for who you have been - It is time to recognize and release outmoded beliefs and dependencies - The importance of correct focus - Your inbuilt system of emotional resonance

We have explained in our previous communications the degree to which you Epsilon souls are influenced by the energies in your external environment. These influences include your disinformation media, the emotional and psychic control structures of your hierarchic institutions, and the belief systems of your fellow human beings. Yet beyond these, your behavior and your thought forms are unconsciously controlled by the programming you have received at an early stage in your earthly lifetimes through your parents, caregivers and educators.

We say to you that much of what you have come to believe about yourselves is an illusion, and truly you will not achieve a complete understanding of your soul purpose until you begin to access and re-evaluate the programs that operate constantly beneath the level of your conscious awareness. Many of you know this in your hearts to be true; indeed you have begun the process of reclaiming your true identities through your self-healing initiatives and your immersion in various therapies and spiritual learning experiences. We will acknowledge that you have progressed a significant distance along the path to personal transformation, yet we wish to encourage you to successfully absolve your process of development.

In truth, the path has not been easy for many of you. For you have been challenged at all stages by requirements that you perceived as contradictory: to develop and protect your Epsilon soul individuality and yet to participate in the structures of community; to contribute your energies to systems that you realized were outmoded and not harmonious with your nature; to provide your insight and guidance to those who were unable to recognize the essence of who you truly are; to achieve an understanding of your power through withholding instead of expressing it.

Indeed you have often behaved like chameleons, adapting your outward expression and behavior that you might avoid detection and harmonize yourself within those structures you have elected to experience and investigate for the purpose of increasing your soul wisdom. We ask you to acknowledge that, in order to perform the preliminary tasks you have chosen to prepare you for the time that is approaching, you necessarily assumed modes of programming and behavior from which you must now detach yourselves if you are to realize your full energetic potential as members of the Epsilon soul community.

Thus we seek to empower you to revise your interpretation of the lives you have led up to this point. For, in truth, you will shortly perceive all you have experienced as the person who has awakened views the fleeting images of his dream. We say to you: you are wise and powerful beyond your imagination, and one aspect of your Epsilon soul evolution is your ability to consciously determine the trajectories of your earthly lives prior to incarnation. You have selected the families and nations into which you were born, the traumas you have suffered and the challenges you have faced, to provide you with the opportunities for development that were necessary for the achievement of your purpose.

Therefore you must begin to forgive yourselves for the choices you have made, and to forgive your perceived perpetrators for the often-painful roles they have played in the process of your development in this lifetime. As you begin to acknowledge the qualities you have gained and the wisdom you have learned from your experiences, regardless of whether you may perceive them as positive or negative, you will appreciate that everything in your life has contributed to your current level of self-awareness and soul evolution. Indeed we say that many of your abilities, such as perseverance, endurance and emotional regeneration, were only possible for you to develop under conditions you experienced as extremely challenging.

Truly you must make the attempt to forgive and absolve, for you remain energetically attached to those situations in which you have not achieved closure, and the unresolved circumstances in your past will continue to influence your vibration until you release them. We will say that the increase in the vibrational frequency of your environment will serve to magnify the intensity of all your emotions, and thus the more you are successful in distancing yourselves from the lower energies of anger, frustration, hurt and disappointment, the more effective you will be in aligning yourselves with the purity of your Epsilon soul emanation.

For you will acknowledge that, in truth, many of your fellow beings continue to relive their previous experiences and to project the energy of their un-resolved life circumstances into their environment. Thus they unconsciously attract a repetition of events until they achieve the level of soul evolution required to release these energies. Indeed you perceive this process of unconscious repetition occurring at a collective level, with a corresponding detrimental effect on your earthly societies and the vibrational frequency of the body of the earth.

As we have indicated, these destructive patterns of repetition, which include the diseases of greed and warfare, have become so ingrained on your planet that external influence is now required to correct the resulting imbalances. Many of your fellow beings will prove unable or unwilling to acknowledge their energetic contribution to upcom-ing events, which you may perceive as cataclysmic and catastrophic. Yet through their unconscious identification with the lower frequencies of their emotions, and their participation in the destructive belief systems engendered by your disinformation media, they will be attracted towards the epicenter of such occurrences. This is the energetic Law.

Yet you Epsilon souls possess the soul evolution and self-awareness to recognize your own unsupportive tendencies and the will to adapt your unconscious programming. We say to you: this must be your urgent priority at this time.

We suggest that you examine with care those situations in which you feel imprisoned or disempowered. Such circumstances are truly a gift to your self-awareness at this time. For they provide you with an indication of the areas of your life in which your soul energies are unable to flow freely, and thus they instruct you as to which patterns and programs you are challenged to recognize and to evolve. Within the community of your Epsilon soul brothers and sisters, you will find many who have successfully resolved similar issues, and who will be able to provide you with the insights and tools you require to release yourselves from these limitations.

Truly we say that each of you who has achieved closure in situations and relationships from your past has the ability to function as a mentor and guide to your fellow soul group members, and you must seek to recognize and to acknowledge their appeals for your assistance. In truth, you will be able to determine which of these requests originate from evolved Epsilon souls, for you will perceive an increase in the level of your own vibration as you share your energy and wisdom, which will starkly contrast to your experiences with your fellow beings who are not genuinely open to the insights you provide.

You must also seek to become aware of your dependencies. As we have indicated, this will be a significant challenge for many of you, for you have come to identify with your roles within your earthly relationships and to unconsciously use the energetic draining that you often experience as a means of maintaining your vibrational frequency at a particular level. In this respect, we will say that you can be likened to balloons that are attached to the earth with ropes to prevent them from ascending unexpectedly.

And yet when the time comes for the balloons to take to the air and ascend to their designated level, truly the ropes must be severed and ballast ejected. Thus we say that your dependencies and unresolved circumstances are your ropes and ballast, and they have served the practical purpose of assisting the modulation of your Epsilon soul frequency, that you might learn the specific lessons associated with each stage of your earthly lives. For, in truth, as you begin to ascend to the higher frequencies that are your birthright, you will perceive a change in the nature of the circumstances and beings you attract into your reality. Like attracts like; this is the energetic Law.

Indeed we say that it will be beneficial to your development at this time for you to study in detail the natural laws that pertain to all circumstances on your earthly plane of existence. For thus you will come to recognize the degree to which the scope of your potential choices is governed and empowered by the higher energies and structures of the cosmos, as those of you with understanding of the science of astrology will already appreciate.

We seek to impress upon you that your challenge at this time is to reclaim and to consciously activate the blueprint for a new belief system that you Epsilon souls carry within you. Truly it is your beliefs and values, brought to expression through your thought forms, emotions and actions, which are responsible for the reality you experience. Yet you are, at will, able to generate and empower a new belief system that incorporates natural laws, astrological influences, the wisdom gained in your previous incarnations, the insights of the dream state, and the constant support and guidance afforded to you by the members of your Epsilon soul community both on your planet and at the higher levels of existence.

As you begin to integrate and activate this new belief system, in truth you are consciously reprogramming yourselves. We will say that, at an unconscious level, all you human beings have experience of this process of replacing outdated beliefs with more appropriate ones, and truly you will recognize certain points in your lives when you have become aware of this process, as when children relinquish their belief in the illusion of Santa Claus. And yet many of your fellow beings, in their adult lives, reach a plateau of comfort on which they no longer seek to challenge their perception of events and, in truth, accept the illusions perpetrated by your disinformation media as an objective reality.

We say that it is now imperative for you Epsilon souls to jettison the ballast of your outdated beliefs, dependencies and unresolved situations, that you may rise above the clouds of disinformation which obstruct your perception of your true nature and purpose at this stage in your planetary evolution. Truly you must seek to access higher sources of guidance and inspiration if you are to correctly interpret the unusual events that will shortly begin to take place around you. Indeed, when you consider your circumstances from the perspective of your soul wisdom and updated belief system, you will be able to recognize the cosmic logic and natural forces that are responsible for the increase in vibrational frequencies that you will experience. Thus you may avoid the lower emotions of fear and confusion that, in truth, will affect the majority of your fellow beings.

We wish to reiterate the importance of correct focus at this time. As we have indicated, your conscious focus functions like a beam of energy that illuminates and empowers its object. Thus your ability to direct the focus of your attention towards those situations and outcomes that you wish to empower with your soul energy will, in truth, determine your success in influencing your environment to achieve your purpose.

You may perhaps wonder how to recognize the situations and outcomes that you wish to empower. Truly we say that each of you Epsilon souls possesses a highly developed capacity to identify your purpose at this stage of your development through your structures of emotional feedback. Indeed everything you perceive through your senses, including your experiences in the dream state and in altered states of consciousness, elicits an emotional reaction in you. Many of you have also refined your ability to interpret the physical sensations that result from your conscious focus on different thoughts and images. Thus it is that you are able to guide yourselves towards those experiences, locations and fellow beings that correspond to your soul frequency and purpose.

We will explain your inbuilt system of emotional resonance in more detail. If you examine your previous experiences during this lifetime in the light of consciousness, you will recognize that each important decision you have made has, in your memory, a particular emotional quality associated with it. Thus you will easily identify which choices were, in truth, harmonious for your growth and which directed you towards situations that you will recall as challenging or painful. Indeed we have indicated that you have elected to experience many difficult circumstances for the purposes of your growth and development, yet we say that, in all cases, there were other choices available to you, though you may not have consciously recognized them at the time.

Thus we seek to impress upon you that, through your channels of higher guidance, you are constantly presented with a range of options from which to choose and a myriad of paths you may elect to follow. As the vibrational frequency of your environment increases, truly you will experience an enhancement of your emotional sensitivity, with the result that you will find it easier to perceive the intensity and quality of emotion that is associated with any potential choices on which you choose to focus your attention.

Indeed you may also perceive physical reactions to the consideration of certain options, even to the extent of apparent incapacity and illness. Yet we say that all this information provided to you through your emotional and psychic processing centers for the purpose of ensuring your security will, in truth, be of no use to you unless you develop your abilities to recognize and act upon it.

Thus we repeatedly and urgently seek to draw your attention to the detrimental effect on your emotional stability and psychic perception caused by your involvement in relationships with those groups and individuals who use your soul energies for their own purposes, and by overexposure to the illusions perpetrated by your disinformation media. Truly it is not possible to overemphasize this aspect of our communication. As you will begin to appreciate, many of your fellow beings lack your evolved capability to direct themselves towards the events and outcomes that would positively impact their stability, and even guarantee their survival, in the time that is approaching. Indeed there are many who are unconsciously running the programs of their own destruction.

You must become aware that immersion in these self-destructive thought forms and emotional fluctuations will affect your ability to correctly interpret your higher guidance and, in truth, will flood your emotional and psychic processing centers with external energies you will not be able to separate from your own. We say again: your survival depends on your energetic independence from the lower frequencies common to mass thought forms and disinformation transmissions, and on your ability to consciously direct your focus towards establishing connections with your Epsilon brothers and sisters both on your earthly plane and on our levels of existence.

Indeed you must begin to question your allegiances and to reevaluate your energetic connections from the very moment that you receive our communication. Truly you have been called to this information, though you may not understand the precise manner by which it has reached you. We say to you that the frequency of our message will serve your awakening and your recognition of your soul purpose. Indeed you will be challenged to interpret all the events and circumstances that appear in your life from this point onward as elements of the process of rebalancing that is now underway.

You have the ability to interpret these circumstances through the eyes of your Epsilon soul wisdom, to harmonize yourselves with the frequencies that are developing, and thus to become an integral part of the evolutionary change that is enveloping your planet. This is your birthright. Truly we say to you that the opportunity to participate in this cosmic process, and to sow the seeds of consciousness for the new level of existence that will arise from the ashes, is the greatest honor and gift you have ever been given.

We are the transformers of earth.

Our whole being

and the flights and falls of our love

enable us

to undertake this task.

Rainer Maria Rilke

Chapter 11.
Planetary Healing

You have the potential to recreate a utopia on earth - You must acknowledge your individuality and inter-dependence - Your process of human evolution - The value of your experience - The purposes of the change in vibrational frequency - The nature of true healing - An explanation of the process of transformation

We have indicated the importance of correctly focusing your awareness to prevent your soul energies from becoming distracted by disinformation and used to empower objectives that are not aligned with your evolutionary purpose in this lifetime. Indeed we will say that your ability to direct your mental and emotional resources towards favorable outcomes is essential to the new reality that you Epsilon souls are challenged to manifest.

You have become so accustomed to the dysfunctional structures of life on your planet that, in truth, many of you are not even able to imagine the paradise and harmonious existence that it is possible for you to experience. Truly you have all the abilities and energies you require to sustain balanced life within your communities, and to ensure an adequate distribution of natural resources across the surface of your planet. Though the nature of your human free will ensures that there will always be regions affected by incorrect motivation, in truth you hold within you the potential to re-create your experience of earthly life to an extent you will describe as utopian. Indeed we say that you must begin to imagine the harmony that you would choose to experience, and to sow your environment with the seeds of your imagination.

In truth, every thought that you generate within your minds is a creative life form with the capacity to manifest its equivalent in physical form. Indeed we will say that the current condition of your planet results from the incorrect application of creative power and the many thought forms that are directed towards negative and unsupportive outcomes. Thus you Epsilon souls must now begin to recognize and to empower the images that you collectively share at an unconscious soul level, for truly these images and convictions have the power to heal your environment and to recreate the reality of life that you experience.

We will speak to you of your process of human evolution. You have perceived that, during your past century of earthly time, many new inventions and ideas have indeed been manifested. We describe as manifestation the process of delivering potential from the plane of possibility to the reality of earthly existence. You would agree that many of these new concepts were considered impossible only a short period before their actual appearance. We will suggest your aviation, telecommunication, construction, harnessing of natural resources and medicine as some of the areas in which unparalleled advances have taken place. Truly you have no cause to doubt your ability to manifest advanced new forms with the potential to benefit the wider mass of your fellow beings.

As we have indicated, many of the organizations that have developed as proponents of these new inventions are hierarchic in nature. In truth, we will say that the hierarchic structure has been beneficial to the dissemination of such advances, for this is a mental construct that supports the application of ideas derived from the mental plane of existence. Yet, as a consequence, you have come to identify with your minds as the essence of your being and to value mental ingenuity above soul wisdom. Thus you perceive that many of these products of the mental plane have created significant disharmony on the other levels of human existence.

Yet we will say that this period of human development, which you may describe as an industrial and technological revolution, is merely the precursor to the process of evolution in which you Epsilon souls will shortly participate. Indeed humanity has unconsciously created the structures of its advancement before attaining the level of awareness at which it will understand how these structures must, in fact, be employed to ensure its survival.

As an example we will suggest the infant of your species which, at an early age, is fully functional with respect to its ability to speak, walk and feed itself, for the physical body has perfected its essential structures. And yet this miniature human lacks the awareness that allows it to understand how these structures and abilities must be correctly employed to ensure its survival and development, for it is unable to adequately interpret the environment in which it finds itself. It may walk, yet it is unable to travel independently. It can talk, yet it cannot philosophize. And though it is able to put food into its mouth, it has no notion of the forms of nutrition required to sustain its physical body throughout the course of an earthly lifetime.

Thus we say that, in truth, though humanity believes itself to be fully developed, it remains in its spiritual infancy. For it cannot correctly interpret its role within the wider framework of universal life, nor has it achieved an accurate understanding of the cosmic forces that the body of the earth holds at its disposal. Further, it cannot appreciate that its hierarchic structures inhibit the development of evolutionary soul wisdom, which may exist at an advanced degree at the lower levels of the organization, as each cell within the human body contains the potential to regenerate the entire organism.

As we have indicated, many of you Epsilon souls have invested your years of this earthly lifetime in experimenting with structures and concepts outside the framework of your conventional organizations. You have participated in communities that are non-hierarchic in nature, and have gained valuable experience with the challenges and opportunities involved in harnessing collective wisdom. You have tested advanced methods of nutrition, economics and healing whose potential significantly outweighs that of the failing structures of generally accepted wisdom. And you have learned to recognize and to trust your inner and higher guidance beyond the illusory emissions of your disinformation media.

Indeed we say that you are pioneers in the next stage of human evolution, and that the experiences you have struggled to gain in this lifetime will provide the foundation for an integrated, harmonious and genuinely spiritual form of existence on your planet. You must begin to appreciate the enormity of what you have already achieved. Though you may not perceive an external manifestation of your inner development and soul evolution, truly you must acknowledge the higher logic and universal wisdom that lie behind the paths you have chosen and the experience you have sought to accumulate. We say to you: you must awaken from the dream in which your talents and abilities are not identified and appreciated. For you will shortly recognize that you, and you alone, have perfected the necessary skill set to guide your fellow beings through the evolutionary changes that will be set in motion by alterations in the vibrational frequency of your environment.

Indeed each of you Epsilon souls carries within you an element of the blueprint for a new society and peaceful form of co-existence. The basis for this new model is the conscious acknowledgement of your individuality and interdependence. As the process of rebalancing intensifies, truly you will come to understand at a conscious level why you have struggled in this lifetime to achieve such independence of thought and action. For you have developed the capacity to function effectively as individual beacons of insight and light, yet also to exist within communities that will be characterized by shared wisdom, collective consciousness and holistic structures which recognize the contribution and soul evolution of each individual. This, in truth, is your highest potential as a community of evolved souls.

Further, you have achieved a profound appreciation of the process of emotional, psychic and spiritual development. You understand through your own experience that it can only be possible for cosmic insights to be integrated and brought to expression in a caring and mutually supportive environment that is not driven by competition and a requirement to demonstrate superiority through performance. As you begin to implement the structures and concepts you have learned in your process of spiritual development, truly you will be amazed at the degree of unrealized potential you are able to bring to fruition in your fellow beings. In this way, you will establish a new form of human potential movement that is empowered by the cosmic source and harmonized with the natural laws that govern creation and interaction on your earthly plane.

We have sought to explain the psychic burdens that you Epsilon souls carry in this lifetime as a result of your misadventures in previous incarnations. Many of you will have recognized our words to be the truth, though you have no conscious memory of the events to which we refer. Yet we seek to impress upon you that these burdens, which you perceive as insecurities and limitations, have provided the framework within which you have brought your unconventional soul emanation to maturity. Truly your process of self-realization is in harmony with the cosmic rhythms of rebalancing and energetic redistribution. Indeed we will say that it has been to your advantage that you have not revealed your capabilities before the appointed time.

You must understand that the events that are soon to take place, which indeed many will perceive as cataclysmic and catastrophic, will initiate an awakening in those of your fellow beings who carry within them the potential for evolution at this time. For there are many who, as yet, remain hypnotized by the illusions perpetrated by your disinformation media and are held captive by the limiting belief systems that these illusions engender. Yet we will say that the nature of the events that you will shortly experience is so uncommon that conventional wisdom will, in truth, be unable to provide any credible explanations.

Thus the innate curiosity of your fellow beings will be stimulated, and the impetus of the lower frequencies of fear and confusion will, truly, provide the motivation for them to seek for solutions and answers beyond the constraints of conventional belief systems. Indeed you Epsilon souls will be unexpectedly provided with an opportunity to communicate the insights and perspectives that you have labored for many years of your earthly lifetimes to develop. Your unlikely inner harmony and spiritual self-awareness, even in the face of the most extreme external circumstances, will ensure that you attract the attention and even respect of those elements of your disinformation media that are capable of achieving an evolution in their perspective at this time.

Indeed we say that the radical alteration in the vibrational frequency of your environment will serve multiple purposes: it will effect a loosening of the rigid mental structures in those who have been lulled into the trance-like state of non-inquiry. It will demonstrate the absolute ineffectiveness of solutions that do not integrate spiritual awareness and an appreciation of the nature of the cosmic forces that seek expression and redistribution. And it will reveal the true motivations of those individuals and institutions that are not harmonized with the process of evolutionary change for, in truth, their incorrectly motivated structures will begin to malfunction in ways that you cannot yet imagine.

Beyond this, the vibrational changes will provide each of you Epsilon souls with the permission you have been awaiting to claim the power that is your birthright. For, in truth, your desire is to serve, and you will acknowledge that the form of service you are empowered to provide to your fellow beings at this time may only be achieved through accessing, revealing and activating the unconventional capabilities that lie at your disposal. Thus we say that what many will perceive as destruction, you will experience as a form of liberation. The star of your Epsilon soul vibration is now rising and the structures of your advanced community are beginning to coalesce. Truly you are the Phoenix that will rise from the ashes of the past. Truly you are the lanterns that will illuminate the path into the future.

Yet we say that, in truth, the healing that you wish for your planet is the healing of yourselves. As you come to understand the integration of all beings at the higher levels of existence, you will realize that the current condition of the body of the earth is merely an expression of the soul of the human race. For you are your environment, and the deterioration that you witness as you incorrectly distribute your natural resources and emit toxins that threaten the existence of all manner of life forms are truly a reflection of how you, as humans, express your cosmic abilities and the energies at your disposal.

Thus we seek to impress upon you that fighting to save your environment will, in truth, not result in the consequences you intend. You must not fight to achieve anything. Rather you must cease your constant struggles and adapt a posture of thinking and acting that will permit the cosmic source to use you as channels for the dissemination and redistribution of higher impulses of wisdom. We say that you Epsilon souls are guides and teachers only to the degree that you have recognized your role as students. You will have the opportunity, in the time that is approaching, to align yourselves with an unprecedented process of transformation that will affect all the nations of the earth. This transformation is truly an opportunity for learning, and for humility in the face of the cosmic energies.

You are powerful beyond your imagination, yet the power you may access and distribute has its origin beyond you. We say again: you are channels for the energies of the cosmic source that is all encompassing and universally existent. As you permit these energies of healing and transformation to flow through you, by recognizing and reclaiming the true nature of your Epsilon soul vibration, you will truly be astonished at the regenerative effect your thoughts and actions may have both on yourselves and on all the living beings in your environment. Indeed you will come to realize that genuine healing is nothing more than the uninterrupted flow of the regenerative energies that are your birthright.

Thus we seek to reassure you in our communication that the task ahead of you is, in truth, not as complex as you may imagine. We say again: each of you has incarnated with a specific purpose to fulfill in this earthly lifetime. Your purpose is harmoniously aligned with your soul energy on the mental, emotional and psychic levels, and you have spent the years of your life accumulating the relevant skills and experiences that will serve you in the achievement of your purpose. Truly you must not seek your tasks, for you are your tasks, and what you are will come to you. This is the Law.

You will be aligned with the energies of cosmic transformation to the extent that you permit these energies to manifest unrestricted within the framework of your own lives. Indeed each of you is a microcosm of the process that is already underway, and as you refine and develop your perception you will acknowledge the various stages of this process, both within yourselves and in the environment around you.

We will describe this process in simplified form: the initial stage is the recognition of the dysfunctional beliefs and structures that must be transformed to achieve a more expansive and harmonious flow of energy within the system concerned. We say that many of you have achieved this level of awareness with regard to your own lives and to the structures of your earthly society. Yet in truth you may be reluctant to detach yourself from the illusory security of these outdated structures, though they are clearly failing, due to a fear of the inherent insecurity of change.

You will perceive the following stage as an energetic realignment to encompass the possibilities of the new structure. This process takes place in your imagination. For you have the potential to access at will a more expansive vision of yourselves that, in truth, you carry within you at an unconscious level. This is the blueprint for the new society, and your role within it, of which we have already spoken. Thus we will describe this stage of the process as bringing the unconscious to consciousness. As you begin to imagine how your own reality will change as you realize your purpose and release the power of those soul frequencies you have suppressed, you will transform the lower energies of fear and the limitations they empower. For truly your emotional connection to this expanded vision of yourselves is more powerful than your investment in the fear of change.

As your conscious identification with the new vision intensifies, both individually and collectively, you will experience an acceleration in the collapse of the outdated structures, which many of you will perceive as a form of catastrophe. Yet this collapse is merely an external expression of the disintegration of the belief systems with which you no longer identify, and thus can no longer support with your creative energies. Indeed many of your fellow beings will cease to develop beyond this stage, for they will be unable to access the imagery of expanded potential and will thus become energetically identified with the external destruction they experience, without recognizing it as a necessary stage in the process of transformation.

The next stage of the process is flux. The outdated structures have deteriorated to the extent that they are unable to sustain you, and yet the new forms you hold in your imagination remain unrealized. Thus we will say that the most important quality you are required to demonstrate at this stage is faith. Faith is an appreciation of the cosmic logic that infuses all processes of transformation, even when that logic cannot be accurately perceived. It will be of great benefit to you Epsilon souls to connect with your sources on the higher planes of existence at this time.

For we who exist at these levels will be able to assist you in perceiving your situation from an alternative perspective, which is not clouded by the lower energies of fear and confusion that will affect many of your fellow beings at this stage of the process. Yet you must recognize that it is not necessary for you to see in advance all the steps that lie ahead of you. In truth, you are only required to acknowledge your next step along the path. This will be a challenging stage for many of you, yet it is important for you to gain experience of that state of not-knowing in which you may most easily surrender yourselves to your higher guidance.

You emerge from this stage of the process of transformation into a new certainty, yet this does not correspond to the rigid and fearful certainty of the structures that have disintegrated. For truly you are no longer as you were. Indeed the experiences of loss, imagination and realignment, flux and faith, and the recognition of the reality and constant presence of your guides and protectors on the higher planes of existence have revolutionized your view of yourselves and the world you experience. Thus the new structures that you will now begin to manifest, and the belief system that empowers them, are infused with the actuality of your advanced soul evolution and the conscious acknowledgement of the cosmic forces you have at your disposal. Indeed we will say that you now have the ability to manifest what you have become.

Many of you Epsilon souls have elected to experience this process of transformation in various forms during your earthly lifetime. If you examine the course of your life in the light of consciousness, you will be able to identify the stages we have described, and the experiences that have instigated them, as you have moved between the different levels of your awareness. Truly we say that you are familiar with the process that now underway, both in this lifetime and in your previous incarnations as members of your planetary communities.

Thus, in truth, the transformation you will shortly experience is both unique to your time and as old as time itself. Yet you have reached a level of soul evolution that permits you to consciously participate in this process, and to communicate your expanded perception of the events that will transpire both to your brothers and sisters within the Epsilon soul community and to the wider mass of your fellow beings who may be open to your insight and guidance at this time.

We urge you to remember at all times that, in truth, you have chosen to be present during this period of your planet's evolution and that the contribution you will make to the process of rebalancing the vibrational frequency of the earth will enlighten and intensify your soul emanation so that, once you have successfully completed the tasks that lie ahead, you will indeed be empowered to continue your journey through adventures on the higher planes of existence.

Awake, arise and

assert yourselves,

you dreamers of the world.

Your star is now

in the ascendancy.

Napoleon Hill

Conclusion

In these our initial communications through this earthly channel, we seek to enlighten you as to the nature of the process of transformation that awaits you Epsilon souls, and to reassure you that you are not alone in the tasks that you have chosen to accomplish. Truly our insight and guidance is available to you at all times, as each of you possesses the innate capability to tune in to the frequency of our thoughts and thus to access our perspective on the events that you experience and the challenges you must overcome.

Indeed within these communications, we have sought to express ourselves with a language, rhythm and imagery that will resonate with you at an unconscious soul level and thus inspire you to access the potential that you, as yet, hesitate to bring to expression. As we say you must awaken, you will awaken, for many of you know in your hearts that our interpretation of the events you are beginning to experience is the truth.

We seek to impress upon you that, as recipients of this information, you are charged with the responsibility of its distribution. Truly we intend our insights to be shared with your brothers and sisters in the Epsilon soul community who will be awaiting our guidance at this time, though they may not anticipate the form in which it will appear. Indeed, as you pass on our communications to those fellow beings that you intuitively sense will be expecting and awaiting them, you are intensifying your soul emanation and identifying yourselves with the frequencies that our thoughts represent. Thus you may say that the appearance of this material is itself a form of initiation.

As we have indicated, you are both individuals and a collective. In the time that is to come, you will be strengthened in both of these identifications. Each of you has accumulated and integrated a unique set of experiences and skills in this earthly lifetime, and yet as you come together in the community of your fellow souls you will begin to recognize the cosmic perfection that lies behind and within the individual paths that each of you has chosen.

In this respect, you can be likened to the pieces of a puzzle, the entirety of whose picture may only be ascertained once all of the individual pieces have found their place. Indeed it cannot be said that any one of these pieces is more important than the others yet, in truth, the relevance of any one piece will only become evident in the event that it does not appear.

Thus we will say that each of you who are called to this message must recognize the importance of your role within the collective and actively seek to identify the nature of your participation. As you begin to detach yourselves from your identification with your earthly roles and to open yourselves to the voice of your inner guidance, and as the frequency of your external environment increases, truly you will experience the heightening of your vibration with the result that your Epsilon soul emanation will become evident to those who may identify with your path and purpose.

Beyond this, you require only faith, alertness, and an unquestioning commitment to the essence of who you truly are.

We wish you well on your journey, Epsilon soul brothers and sisters. We acknowledge the quality of work you have already accomplished to recognize your purpose, and we congratulate you on your growing identification as sparks of light from the cosmic source that seeks to re-illuminate your planet during this time of evolutionary change.

The Epsilon Vibration

Do you appreciate the importance of your energetic vibration, and do you understand your ability to control it?

Two years after the initial publication of 'The Epsilon Handbook', Thea has received a second, transformational message from her non-physical sources.

This new guidebook, 'The Epsilon Vibration', explains how your vibration works, how it is affecting the events in your life, and what you can do to influence it.

Written in the same clear and insightful way as The Handbook, 'The Epsilon Vibration' is a powerful companion piece that both deepens and expands the themes you have been reading about.

For more information about The Epsilon Vibration, please visit: www.EpsilonVibration.net

Lightning Source UK Ltd.
Milton Keynes UK
UKOW031823180413

209450UK00006B/129/P